EMAILS
Fwd: FW:

EMAILS
Fwd: FW:

THE DIFFERENCE
COMMUNICATION GENERATION

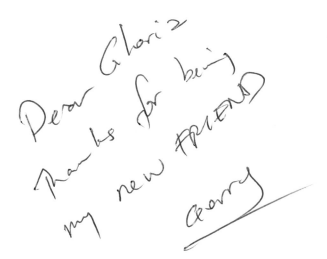

Dear Gloria
Thanks for being
my new FRIEND
Gerry

Gerry Gialogo
Grindulo

To order additional copies of this book, contact:
Xlibris Corporation
1-888-795-4274
www.Xlibris.com
Orders@Xlibris.com
56328

CONTENTS

INVITATION

To share your story in my next book entitled: 'In Search Of The Difference'.

Throughout history, some people have wanted to make a change; to make a difference. Change has brought us equality between all human beings, of all colors, and of all sexes. Change has given humanity the complex society we live in today. No one has the same beliefs, lifestyles, likes or dislikes. As this may sound as a negative aspect as to what people have become, we must think of this as evolution of mankind. We are all equal, but different.

That is why I must invite you, all of you, to share your stories of making a difference. Whether it may be a person, a thing, a time, a place, a moment, an event, a reason, an idea, or anything that may have altered your life or may have effect on someone else's life, please share your story through my next book, because any story is a great story.

Many would want to hear stories of love, success, faith, health, relationships, family, failure, fame, fortune or tragedy, because these are parts of everyone's life that creates change in themselves. These types of events, actions, or people have brought other through thick, through thin, and everything in between. It is these events, actions, or people that have molded others as to who they are today.

Merriam-Webster defines difference by "a significant change or effect on a situation." Wouldn't you want your act of making a difference to be heard? Wouldn't you want to make a difference in someone else's life? Giving each other motivation and inspiration is the first and most important step when helping a fellow friend. And sharing your story is what you can do.

The book is intended to start a *Library of Personal Stories . . .* from all over the world.

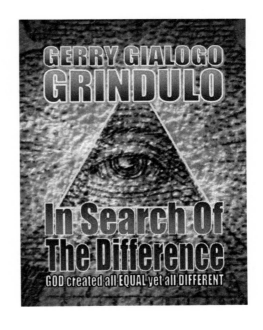

GERRY GIALOGO GRINDULO

In Search Of The Difference

GOD created all EQUAL yet all DIFFERENT

E-mail your story to: *Gerry@Grindulo.com* with your NAME, ADDRESS, GENDER, AGE, PHONE NUMBER, TITLE OF YOUR STORY, FICTITIOUS NAME (if desired) and a brief description of yourself.

Contributors will enjoy wholesalers' discount with no minimum or maximum order. If your story is voted *The Best Story* by the readers, you will win a share of the royalty of the book.

Submitting your story means that you agree that *The Difference* assume full rights of the stories submitted.

You don't have to pay anything to publish your story—just enjoy all the benefits.

Please share this invitation to anyone you know who might be interested. Thank you.

To Our Legacy,

Gerry G. Grindulo
Author and Founder of *The Difference*

INVITATION

To share your story in my next book entitled: 'Little Gears That Make The Difference'

If you are an entrepreneur, you are invited to share your story about your business in my next book *Little Gears That Make the Difference*. This book will connect principled entrepreneurial heroes with the world—a connection that has unlimited potential. It will reshape paradigms and will ignite new ideas. Your adventure called entrepreneurship is a journey that helps change the world. The communities and the world are the beneficiaries of your great business minds. You are truly heroes who inspire and instill virtues.

Share your venture, your main products or services, when you started, number of employees, your mission, struggles, challenges, sacrifices you faced and how you overcame them, and key lessons you learned from your business. Let the next generation gain wisdom from your wealth of knowledge. As a living hero and a legend to your employees, associates, and clients, you deserve a little more fame. This book is also your best way to recognize the people who help you plan and work through the setbacks and roadblocks.

Your business is you personified. You are a brilliantly unique person with values, passion, and an ability to grow your company over the years . . . through an assortment of twists and turns . . . calling for strength, tenacity, and endless determination. With integrity and purpose, your endeavor provides deep fulfillment, a sense of gratitude, and a contribution to the world at large. The world is waiting to hear this story.

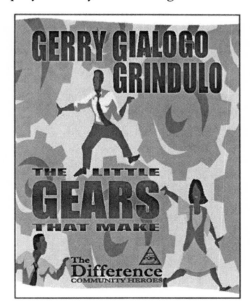

In the end, everyone would like to leave a legacy that documents realization of dreams and vision. It is time for you to take that step. The book will enable you to pass on the torches of knowledge, wisdom, and insight to the next generation, creating your legacy that will change lives, change the world, give inspiration to the aspiring entrepreneurs who follow in your footsteps, and assist the ones who have a dream but lack a guide. That guide may be you. And so, the journey continues. Let us pass on your story. Make a difference.

E-mail your story to: *Gerry@Grindulo.com* with your NAME, ADDRESS, GENDER, AGE, PHONE NUMBER, TITLE OF YOUR STORY, and BUSINESS NAME.

Contributors will enjoy wholesalers' discount with no minimum or maximum order. If your story is voted *The Best Story* by the readers, you will win a share of the royalty of the book.

Submitting your story means that you agree that *The Difference* assume full rights of the stories submitted.

This book is a lifetime marketing promotion for your company, the best gift you can give to your customers and friends, and an additional profitable item you may sell in stores.

Please share this invitation to anyone you know who might be interested. Thank you.

To Our Legacy,

Gerry G. Grindulo
Author and Founder of The Difference

INVITATION

To share your story in my next book entitled: 'We, the People . . . The Difference, Then and Now'

Since the time that you can remember, your life has evolved. Like everyone else, it has its peaks and valleys. To some, it is even like a roller-coaster ride. Events are happening too fast to keep up with. To some it is like a ride on a paddle boat on a serene lake. Movement is very slow, peaceful, or even boring.

Whatever kind of life we had in the past, it sure did change for better or worst. Did your beliefs changed? How about your lifestyle? Are you financially better off now or were you better before? Do you have more friends now or before? How did relationships affect your life? If you are a business person, is your business doing better now or before? What about the government? Do you think the government programs benefited you or made your life worst?

I believe that there are millions of stories there to be shared. Stories about good life from bad and stories about bad life from good.

And so I must invite you to share your stories about anything that may have altered your life. You'll never know, your story might save someone's life by learning a lesson from yours.

Faith, love, fame, fortune, success, failure, health, relationships, tragedy, and other special moments and events changed our life and molded us into who we are today . . . We, the People . . . The Difference in our life between Then and Now.

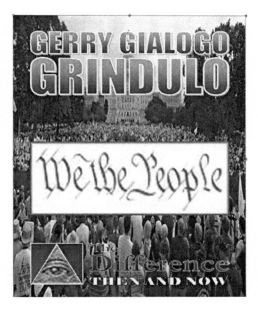

The book is intended to start a Library of Personal Stories—from all over the world.

E-mail your story to: *Gerry@ Grindulo.com* with your NAME, ADDRESS, GENDER, AGE,

PHONE NUMBER, TITLE OF YOUR STORY, FICTITIOUS NAME (if desired) and a brief description of yourself.

Contributors will enjoy wholesalers' discount with no minimum or maximum order. If your story is voted *The Best Story* by the readers, you will win a share of the royalty of the book.

Submitting your story means that you agree that *The Difference* assume full rights of the stories submitted.

You don't have to pay anything to publish your story—just enjoy all the benefits.

Please share this invitation to anyone you know who might be interested. Thank you.

To Our Legacy,

Gerry G. Grindulo
Author and Founder of The Difference

In Loving Memory

In Loving Memory of my dad, *Greg*
Who kept our family very close together . . .
And even closer together . . .
After he passed away . . .

DEDICATION

TO

MY JOYOUS BEAUTIFUL WIFE	*Susan*
OUR GODSENT CHILDREN	*Toto . Mitch . Jodi*
MY EXCEPTIONAL BROTHER, MY DEVOTED SISTERS, & REMARKABLE FAMILY	*Dan . Lovely . Danda . Dandoy* *Neng . John . Roselene . Annie . Junior* *Che . Roy* *Joy . Melvin . Kristina* *Jing-Jing*
ALL GRACIOUS	*Gialogos & Grindulos* *Friends & Relatives* *Clients & Colleagues*

AND MOST OF ALL . . . TO

OUR WONDROUS BELOVED MOM   *Rose*

I DEDICATE THIS BOOK.

ACKNOWLEDGMENTS

To all those who forwarded their emails to me . . . you have validated your purpose of entertaining, educating, informing, involving, tricking, motivating, enlightening, cautioning, and sharing with me wonderful articles. I consider such act as a gesture of making me part of your daily life, continuously communicating with me, the way we communicate in this modern times;

To Phil Johnson, Ross Plaza, Ashley Nuico, Lynn Chavez, Lani Meyer, Ally Field, Karen Almendra, Tara Lungay, and Gail Lim . . . you did a good job publishing this book;

To Roy Enriquez . . . you spent valuable hours and demonstrated technical expertise in fixing the computer I used to make this book;

To those who did not believe the success of this endeavor . . . you opened stimulating and challenging discussions . . . you extended my contextual horizon and provided me the gear to accelerate in finishing what I have started;

To my sons Gregg Girard and Josef Mitchell, my pride and joy . . . you provided continuous support, watchful eye to its development, and vital assistance in publishing this book; and

To MY FAMILY: my wife, my brother and sisters and their better halves, and all our children, and most of all, our beloved Mom who dedicated every beat of her heart to her children . . . you all are my strength, my purpose, and my inspiration.

Preface

It is almost 30 years ago when I first came to the U.S. from the Philippines. Although coming to America made my future looks promising, it was the most sacrificial move I have ever done. All I wanted to do when I first arrived into America was to talk to my mom, my brother, my sisters, and all my loved ones.

Kids today may not realize how emotionally taxing it was then to go to other countries leaving your loved ones behind. Back then, it was uncertain how and when we are going to see and talk to each other again.

Communication then was very different as compared to now. Back then, the only forms of communication available to the general public is the postal mail and the telephone, with the exception of telegraph or telex which is used mostly for emergency or business purposes because of the high cost.

Mails thru the post office which we now call the "snail mail" was very slow. To send a regular mail to the Philippines would take about a month or more to get there. It also takes the same amount of time to receive the reply. So, for my questions written and sent through mail, I would have to wait about two months to get the answers.

I would watch out for friends who are traveling to the Philippines and ask a favor of bringing my mails so my loved ones will receive news about me faster. Likewise, my loved ones also look for people going to the U.S. to bring their mails so I'll be able to receive their reply faster than sending through the post office. It was the quickest possible way to communicate by mail, unless, of course, we use the telephone which is very expensive.

Long distance telephone rate was very high. The telephone industry then was not deregulated yet. For me to make a long distance phone call to the Philippines, I would have to pay 10 US dollars for the first 3 minutes, then 2 US dollars for every additional minute. So for a 20 minute call, I would need 44 US dollars plus the taxes and other phone company charges. But for a big family with a lot of members who wanted to hear each other and missing each other very much, with a lot of story everyone wants to tell, an hour or two is not even enough. There are occasions when we sacrifice a week or a month worth of earnings to be able to communicate to each other.

Coming from a country like the Philippines, a dollar means a lot for us. Especially for poor people, a dollar means food for a family for several days. Others just give up communications affecting their relationships because of its cost.

And then, one day, communication evolved. The world has become a lot smaller now. Missing someone now means entirely different as missing someone then.

About 20 years ago, I was introduced to electronic mail, we now call "emails", mails that can be sent and received anywhere in the world almost instantaneously by the touch of fingers on a keyboard, made possible by the miraculous internet.

Back then, email was restricted to only text. But thanks to the standard of ARPANET (Advanced Research Projects Agency Network), emails have been top-notched from the get-go.

The world has gone through many transitions as to how everyone communicates. They have sent messengers to relay information, smoke signals, Morse code, and even beating a drum was a form of communication.

Now, the day-to-day forms of communication have become the internet, the mobile phone, and faster postal mail. We can thank technology for making it better for all of us to communicate with one another. People from around the world can now send pictures, wire money, or even video chat with family, friends, and even strangers. These forms of communication made this gigantic world seem so much smaller and made us closer together.

My dream had come true. I can communicate with my loved ones as if they were next to me. It had become easy to keep each other up-to-date as to how everyone is doing and whatnot.

Later, after I had been introduced to the internet and email, loved ones and even people I barely know started sending me mails. I've received personal mails, stories, news, and even jokes from around the world.

This began a chain of emails being sent to me from my family and friends. Soon or later, I began to receive mails from my family's friends, my friends' friends, and before I knew it, I had collected hundreds, if not thousands of emails. There are stories about love, stories about faith, stories about relationships, stories about emotions, moral-filled stories, and other different kind of stories.

Throughout time, I was able to read every single one of the stories sent to me. Some of those stories had shared shaping me. Some stories provided me strength. Some stories had given me endurance, so that I may endure the long path of bringing my loved ones to America. Some stories were a reminder that when times are hard, I can rest my head on my faith. Almost every story that had been given me had made me better in different ways.

The following contents of this book had helped shaped and formed my life. It had changed me in ways that I have never thought words would. That is why I have decided to compile the works of various writers, some known, some unknown, so that there may be a chance that these words may make a difference in you.

Things Nice to Know About Email and Email Forwarding

Before you start reading the articles I am forwarding through this book, you might want to know some information about email and email forwarding.

Let us take a look as to what it really is, how and when this written communications evolve, and how one should properly create, send, and of course, forward emails.

According to Wikipedia, **electronic mail**, often abbreviated as **email** or **e-mail**, is a method of exchanging digital messages, designed primarily for human use. E-mail systems are based on a store-and-forward model in which e-mail computer server systems accept, forward, deliver and store messages on behalf of users, who only need to connect to the e-mail infrastructure, typically an e-mail server, with a network-enabled device (e.g., a personal computer) for the duration of message submission or retrieval. Rarely is e-mail transmitted directly from one user's device to another's.

An electronic mail message consists of two components, the message *header*, and the message *body*, which is the email's content. The message header contains control information, including, minimally, an originator's email address and one or more recipient addresses. Usually additional information is added, such as a subject header field.

During the 1960's and 1970's many companies who were using mainframe and mini computers also used email facilities on those systems. This enabled users of terminals attached to those systems to send messages to each other. As companies began to connect their central systems (hosts) to branch offices and subsidiaries then employees were able to send email to other employees of that company on a world-wide basis.

Also during this time the US Department of Defense's research into computer networks was well underway, resulting in the embryonic ARPANET—the forerunner to the now global INTERNET. According to information regarding these early years, the first ARPANET network email message was transmitted in 1971.

In the late 1970's and 1980's the phenomenal growth of personal computers created a whole new genre of email technologies. Some of these systems were proprietary 'dial-up' systems. For two people to exchange messages remotely on these systems they had to both be subscribers. The proprietary systems did not interoperate or transmit messages from one system to another.

Since 1995 both the Internet and email have been 'hot' topics. But when one cuts away the hype, one realizes that email itself is not new. What is relatively new however is that email is now: more readily available interoperable between systems

No doubt the Internet will shape future communications, far beyond the current uses. As to what features and functions that will become available over the next few years, the speed of progress dictates that we can only guess.

Email and Email Forwarding Etiquette

Emailing and email forwarding can be as formal or as informal as you like, whichever you please. But if you are concerned about your e-mailing etiquette, here's a little info you might want to know. This might prevent you from embarrassing yourself at some point in the near future.

- Use the 'To' only for addresses you want to direct your message. Otherwise, the receivers have no clue as to who should take action so either they all do something or they all do nothing.

- Use the 'Cc' only for addresses you think will find the message relevant. Do not always copy your entire address book. Some receivers may think that you are 'crying for attention'.

- Use the 'Bcc' for addresses you don't want other receivers to see. This will prevent receivers of your email from sending messages to addresses in the 'Bcc'.

- The 'Reply to All' button is just a button, but it can generate tons of unnecessary e-mails. For example, if I send a dozen people an e-mail asking if they are available at a certain time for a meeting I should get a dozen replies and that's it. However, if each person hits the "Reply to All' button not only do I get a dozen replies, but so does everyone else for a total of 144 messages! I'm not saying that the 'Reply to All' button should not be used. I'm saying that it should be used with care.

- Messages should be concise and to the point. It's also important to remember that some people receive hundreds of e-mail messages a day.

- Don't forward without editing out email addresses, headers and commentary from all the other forwarders. If you must forward, only forward the actual content of the email that in your opinion is valuable.

- If you cannot take the time to write a personal comment at the top of your forwarded email to the person you are sending to—then you shouldn't forward it at all.

- Be sure that what you are forwarding will be of value with accurate information. Check for hoaxes @ Snopes.com.

- Be sure what you are forwarding is something the recipient needs. If it is humorous, think if your recipients have the same sense of humor as you do. If you cannot think of why the person you are forwarding to would like to receive the email—then don't forward it.

- If on company time using company e-mail, think not twice, but more times. Ask yourself if forwarding is worth the risk of your job credibility and professionalism.

- Forwarding of chain letters; regardless how noble the topic may seem, virus warnings or anything that says "forward to everyone you know" simply shouldn't be forwarded.

- If you must forward to more than one person, put your email address in the TO: field and all the others you are sending to in the BCC: field. Do not continue to forward those visible addresses to your contacts! Remove any email addresses in the body of the email.

- When it comes to receiving unwanted forwarded emails, if you fear hurting someone's feelings by asking them to stop forwarding you email and you know they meant well, then just hit delete!

- Don't get caught up in grammar and punctuation, especially excessive punctuation. Do not put a dozen exclamation points at the end of a sentence for added emphasis. Exclamation points are just another form of ending a sentence. If something is important it should be reflected in your text, not in your punctuation.

- Formatting can be everything, but not here. Plain text is it. Do not format messages so that they have fancy fonts, or colors. There are lots of e-mail clients which cannot handle messages in these formats.

- Back in dial-up days I would have recommended that all attachments be held to 1MB in size. For users on broadband or a direct connection, I would up the limit to 5MB. HOWEVER, the only time I send attachments of the 5MB size is when I know the other party expects it.

- Nothing is more wasteful than to reply to an e-mail by including a complete copy of the original with the words "I agree", "Okay" or "Ditto" at the bottom.

- Personal e-mails sent from the office are regarded as official company communications regardless of content and could possibly expose you and your company to unnecessary risk.

- Use of upper-case words is the equivalent of shouting in some one's ear. ONLY use upper-case words when trying to make a point (such as I just did). Even at that, you should be careful with who you are exchanging messages.

- Do not make a comment about grammar or punctuation. Nobody wants to feel like they are exchanging e-mail with their eighth-grade English teacher.

- Do not send a mass-mailing advertisement unless authorized by the receivers

- With e-mail you send a message and then wait for a response. The response may come in five minutes or the response may come in five days. Either way it's not an interactive conversation. Too many users assume that the minute someone receives an e-mail, the person will read it. That is a bad assumption. If you schedule a meeting for an hour from now and send an e-mail to each attendee, the chance that all the attendees will read that message within the hour will be pretty small. On the other hand, if you schedule the meeting for the next day, the chance that they will read the message will be pretty high. Remember, e-mail is not designed for immediacy (that's why you have a telephone), it's designed for convenience.

- Abbreviation usage is quite rampant with e-mail. In the quest to save keystrokes, users have traded clarity for confusion (unless you understand the abbreviations). I would recommend that you use abbreviations that are already common to the English language, such as 'FYI' and 'BTW'. Beyond that, you run the risk of confusing your recipient. Some of the more common abbreviations are listed in the table below.

THIS	MEANS THIS
o BCNU	be seeing you
o BTW	by the way
o FWIW	for what it's worth
o FYI	for your information
o IMHO	in my humble opinion
o OBO	or best offer
o ROTFL	rolling on the floor laughing

- o RTFM   read the funny manual
- o TNSTAAFL   there's no such thing as a free lunch
- o TTFN   ta ta for now
- o TTYL   talk to you later

Smilies

Having trouble expressing your emotions over an e-mail? It might be a little difficult when your recipient can only see words. But not for long! Computer users throughout time have developed fun and innovative ways to express your facial expressions. Here's a taste of how you can express your emotions without lengthy context.

THIS	MEANS THIS
:-)	smiley face
;-)	wink (light sarcasm)
:-|	indifference
:->	devilish grin (heavy sarcasm)
8-)	eyeglasses
:-D	shock or surprise
:-/	perplexed
:-(	frown (anger or displeasure)
:-P	wry smile
;-}	leer
:-Q	smoker
:-e	disappointment
:-@	scream
:-O	yell
:-*	drunk
:-{}	wears lipstick

Email as a wonderful tool is not without its downside. A virus email that infect and damage computers can often be very difficult to detect. If you received an anonymous email then you may not want to open it. The mere act of opening the email makes your computer susceptible to infection. Privacy has also become an issue with email. Virtually every email has to go through a number of computers before it reaches the inbox of the intended receiver. There is a distinct chance that someone could hack into your email. It is important that you have an anti-virus protection.

A Brief Introduction of the Following Content

When I began pulling together the contents of this book, I found it very important that the book should be separated into multiple sections that I feel is important to all people around the world. From faith to family, humor to health, each and every subject involved here takes part in every single person's lives. That is why I believe this book, *EMAILS Fwd: FW* can be a guide for anyone.

I sat in front of my writing instrument for hours, trying to figure out how in the world I would introduce a book such as this. I could speak aimlessly about how this book has stories about this, or this book has stories about that. However, I believe that an introduction like that is a waste of printing. Just read the book.

But if I were to say something about this book before you begin, I would just like to say that this world is an interesting and crazy world. Many of the stories compiled in this book are either non-fiction stories, or fiction stories that are based on what could happen in the real world. Although I can easily state that I have not seen everything in this world, the contents of this book gives me an idea of what occurs around me, and it gives me perspective as to how I view the world. And let me tell you; the world does not confine to what you want or what you need. We all are not here to be catered and taken cared of, but we need to live for ourselves . . . survival of the fittest, so to speak.

Disclaimer

When I began creating this book, I went in with the realization that there could potentially be a problem with the contents of this book. The majority of these words that are printed in this book are not mine, and I do not intend to claim so. I believe that every artist should be accredited for any work they do. Drawings, writings, pictures, songs, or other forms . . . everyone deserves their name out there unless, of course, they don't want to.

This book is a compilation of works from authors that are known and unknown. Please note that anyone who feels they are being copyrighted in any part of this book, please contact me immediately so that this book can give credit where it is due. I did not plan on stealing stories, jokes, notes, or any text from any author. The stories were given to me as is, with or without author or writer. Remember, these are forwarded e-mails. Accreditation can be lost throughout such long chain mails and whatnot.

If you find any of your work throughout this book and would like to receive credit, please contact me so I may do so.

As a reminder, I want to state that this book is not mine. It is not my family's book. It is not the publisher's book. This book is for everyone and *is* everyone's. I would like to thank those in advance for contributing to what can potentially change the views of many in the world.

ABOUT ART

Paintings of Vincent Van Gogh with Lyrics of Don McLean's Starry, Starry, Night

Starry, starry night,
Paint your palette blue and grey.

Look out on a summer's day
with eyes that know the darkness in my soul.

Shadows on the hills,

sketch the trees and the daffodils,
catch the breeze and the winter chills

in colors on the snowy linen land.

Now I understand

what you tried to say to me,

how you suffered for your sanity,

how you tried to set them free.

Starry, starry night,

flaming flowers that brightly blaze,

swirling clouds in violet haze
reflect in Vincent's eyes of China blue

Colors changing hue,

morning fields of amber grain,

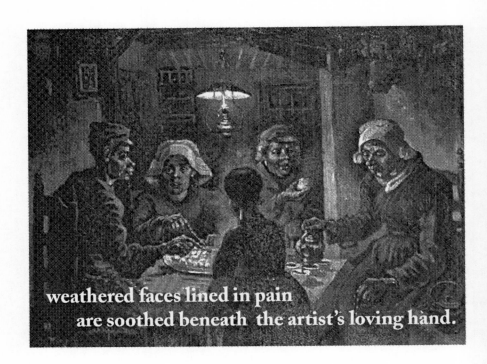

weathered faces lined in pain
are soothed beneath the artist's loving hand.

Now I understand

what you tried to say to me,
how you suffered for your sanity,
how you tried to set them free.

They would not listen.
They did not know how.
Perhaps they'll listen now.

For they could not love you,

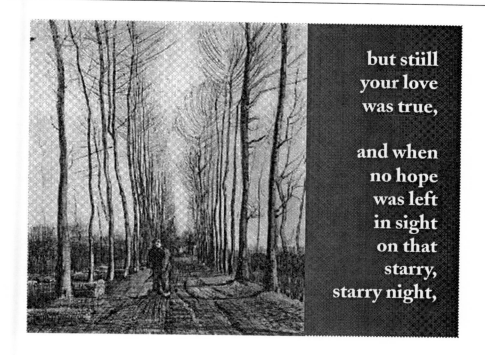

but stiill
your love
was true,

and when
no hope
was left
in sight
on that
starry,
starry night,

You took your life as lovers often do;

But I could have told you, Vincent,
this world was never meant
for one as beautiful as you.

Starry, starry night,

portraits hung in empty halls,

frameless heads on nameless walls,

with eyes that watch the world and can't forget.

Like the strangers that you've met,

the ragged men in ragged clothes,

the silver thorn of bloody rose
lie crushed and broken on the virgin snow.

Now I think I know what you tried to say to me,

how you suffered for your sanity,

how you tried to set them free.

They would not listen.
They're not list'ning still.

ABOUT EMERGENCY

CAR KEYS

With Electronic Car Door Opener

Good use for car keys! (The electronic car door opener)

Put your car keys beside your bed at night. If you hear a noise outside your home or someone is trying to get into your house, just press the panic button for your car. The alarm will be set off, and the horn will continue to sound until either you turn it off or the car battery dies.

This tip came from a neighborhood watch coordinator. Next time you come home for the night and you start to put your keys away, think of this; it's a security alarm system that you probably already have and requires no installation.

Test it. It will go off from almost anywhere inside your house and will keep honking until your battery runs down or until you reset it with the button on the key chain. It works if you park in your driveway or garage.

If your car alarm goes off when someone is trying to break into your house, odds are the burglar or rapist won't stick around. After a few seconds, all the neighbors will be looking out their windows to see who is out there and sure enough the criminal won't want that.

And remember to carry your keys while walking to your car in a parking lot. The alarm can work the same way there. This is something that should really be shared with everyone. Maybe it could save a life or a sexual abuse crime.

I think it is fantastic. Would also be useful for any emergency, such as a heart attack, where you can't reach a phone. My mom has suggested to my dad that he carries his car keys with him in case he falls outside, and she doesn't hear him. He can activate the car alarm and then she'll know there's a problem.

HEART ATTACK

Let's say it's 6.15pm and you're
driving home (alone of course) after
an unusually hard day on the job.
You're really tired, and
frustrated......

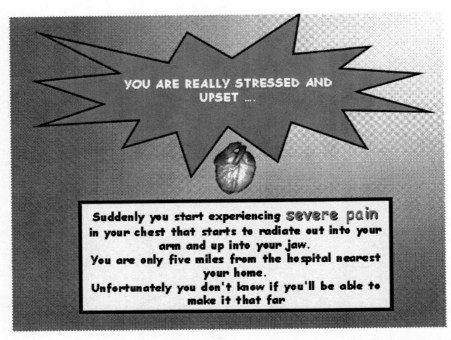

HOW TO SURVIVE A HEART ATTACK WHEN ALONE?

SINCE MANY PEOPLE ARE ALONE WHEN THEY SUFFER A HEART ATTACK, WITHOUT HELP, THE PERSON WHOSE HEART IS BEATING IMPROPERLY AND WHO BEGINS TO FEEL FAINT, HAS ONLY ABOUT 10 SECONDS LEFT BEFORE LOSING CONSCIOUS

WHAT TO DO ??

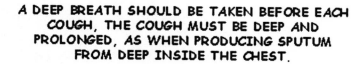

ANSWER:

DO NOT PANIC, BUT START COUGHING REPEATEDLY AND VERY VIGOROUSLY.

A DEEP BREATH SHOULD BE TAKEN BEFORE EACH COUGH, THE COUGH MUST BE DEEP AND PROLONGED, AS WHEN PRODUCING SPUTUM FROM DEEP INSIDE THE CHEST.

A BREATH AND A COUGH MUST BE REPEATED ABOUT EVERY TWO SECONDS WITHOUT LET-UP UNTIL HELP ARRIVES, OR UNTIL THE HEART IS FELT TO BE BEATING NORMALLY AGAIN.

DEEP BREATHS GET OXYGEN INTO THE LUNGS AND COUGHING MOVEMENTS SQUEEZE THE HEART AND KEEP THE BLOOD CIRCULATING. THE SQUEEZING PRESSURE ON THE HEART ALSO HELPS IT REGAIN NORMAL RHYTHM. IN THIS WAY, HEART ATTACK VICTIMS CAN GET TO A HOSPITAL

ARTICLE PUBLISHED ON N.º 240 OF *JOURNAL OF GENERAL HOSPITAL ROCHESTER*

TELL AS MANY OTHER PEOPLE AS POSSIBLE ABOUT THIS.
IT COULD SAVE THEIR LIVES !!! DON'T EVER THINK THAT YOU ARE NOT PRONE TO HEART ATTACK AS YOUR AGE IS LESS THAN 25 OR 30. NOWADAYS DUE TO THE CHANGE IN THE LIFE STYLE, HEARTATTACK IS FOUND AMONG PEOPLE OF ALL AGE GROUPS.

BE A FRIEND AND PLEASE SEND THIS ARTICLE TO AS MANY FRIENDS AS POSSIBLE

ICE
(In Case of Emergency)

We all carry our mobile phones with names and numbers stored in its memory but nobody, other than ourselves, knows which of these numbers belong to our closest family or friends.

If we were to be involved in an accident or were taken ill, the people attending us would have our mobile phone but wouldn't know who to call. Yes, there are hundreds of numbers stored, but which one is the contact person in case of an emergency?

Hence this ICE (In Case of Emergency) Campaign.

The concept of ICE is catching on quickly. It is a method of contact during emergency situations. As cell phones are carried by the majority of the population, all you need to do is store the number of a contact person or persons who should be contacted during emergency under the name ICE (In Case Of Emergency).

The idea was thought up by a paramedic who found that when he went to the scenes of accidents, there were always mobile phones with patients, but they didn't know which number to call. He therefore thought that it would be a good idea if there were a nationally recognized name for this purpose. In an emergency situation, Emergency Service personnel and hospital Staff would be able to quickly contact the right person by simply dialing the number you have stored as ICE.

For more than one contact name, simply enter ICE1, ICE2, and ICE3 etc. A great idea that will make a difference!

Let's spread the concept of ICE by storing an ICE number in our mobile phones today! Some newer models of mobile phones already have the ICE feature in the contact list.

Needle Can Save the Life of a Stroke Victim

from a Chinese Professor (Irene Liu)

Keep a syringe or needle in your home to do this. It's amazing and an unconventional way of recovering from stroke, read it through it can help somebody one day.

This is amazing. Please keep this very handy. Excellent tips. Do take a minute to read this. You'll never know, someone's life may depend on you.

My father was paralyzed and later died from the result of a stroke. I wish I knew about this *first aid* before.

When stroke strikes, the capillaries in the brain will gradually burst.

When a stroke occurs, stay calm.

No matter where the victim is, do not move him/her. Because if moved the capillaries will burst.

Help the victim to sit up where he/she is to prevent him/her from falling over again and then the bloodletting can begin.

If you have in your home an injection syringe, that would be the best.

Otherwise, a sewing needle or a straight pin will do.

1. Place the needle over fire to sterilize it and then use it to prick the tip of all ten fingers.
2. There are no specific acupuncture points, just prick about an mm from the fingernail.
3. Prick till blood comes out.
4. If blood does not start to drip, then squeeze with your fingers.
5. When ten fingers are bleeding, wait for a few minutes for the victim to regain consciousness.
6. *If the victim's mouth is crooked*, then pull on his ears until they are red.
7. Then prick each earlobe twice until two drops of blood comes from each earlobe. After a few minutes, the victim should regain consciousness.

Wait till the victim regains his normal state without any abnormal symptoms and then take him to the hospital. Otherwise, if he was taken in the ambulance in a hurry to the hospital, the bumpy trip will cause all the capillaries in his brain to burst.

If he could save his life, barely managing to walk, then it is by the grace of his ancestors.

I learned about letting blood to save life from Chinese traditional doctor, Ha Bu Ting, who lives in Sun Juke.

Furthermore, I had practical experience with it. Therefore, I can say this method is 100 percent effective.

In 1979, I was teaching in Fung Gaap College in Tai Chung.

One afternoon, I was teaching a class when another teacher came running to my classroom *and said in panting, "Ms. Liu, come quick, our supervisor has had a stroke!"*

I immediately went to the third floor. When I saw our supervisor, Mr. Chen Fu Tien, he looked pale, his speech was slurred, his mouth was crooked—all the symptoms of a stroke.

I immediately asked one of the practicum students to go to the pharmacy outside the school to buy a syringe, which I used to prick Mr. Chen's ten fingers tips.

When all ten fingers were bleeding (each with a pea-sized drop of blood), after a few minutes, Mr. Chen's face regained its color and his eyes' spirit returned,

But his mouth was still crooked. So I pulled on his ears to *fill them with blood.*

When his ears became red, I pricked his *right earlobe* twice to let out two drops of blood. When *both earlobes* had two drops of blood each, a miracle happened. Within three to five minutes the shape of his mouth returned to normal and his speech became clear.

We let him rest for a while and have a cup of hot tea, then we helped him go down the stairs, drove him to Wei Wah Hospital. He rested one night and was released the next day to return to school to teach. Everything worked normally. There were no ill aftereffects.

On the other hand, the usual stroke *victim usually suffers irreparable bursting of the brain capillaries on the way to the hospital.* As a result, these victims never recover. Stroke is the second cause of death. The lucky ones will stay alive but can remain paralyzed for life.

It is such a horrible thing to happen in one's life.

If we can all remember this blood letting method and start the life saving process immediately, in a short time, the victim will be revived and regain 100 percent normality.

PIN NUMBER REVERSAL
(GOOD TO KNOW)

If you have and use an ATM Card to withdraw money and you're being forced to get cash for an invader, you may want to know this! I was skeptical about this one and called The Bank of America to verify it. They told me it is true; it's something that has evolved fairly recently.

If you should ever be forced by a robber to withdraw money from an ATM machine, you can notify the police by entering your Pin # in reverse.

For example, if your pin number is 1234 then you would put in 4321 The ATM recognizes that your pin number is backward from the ATM card you placed in the machine.

The machine will still give you the money you requested, but unknown to the robber, the police will be immediately dispatched to help you.

This information was recently broadcasted on FOX TV, and it states that it is seldom used because people don't know it exists.

STR
(SMILE, TALK, RAISE ARMS)

Very Important To Know about *Stroke*

Remember the first three letters—S, T, R—(You may have seen this before, but . . . this is important!) My friend sent this to me and encouraged me to post it and spread the word. I agree. If everyone can remember something this simple, we could save some folks. Seriously—an ounce of prevention is a pound of cure; please read.

Stroke Identification: During a BBQ, a friend stumbled and took a little fall; she assured everyone that she was fine (they offered to call paramedics) and just tripped over a brick because of her new shoes. They got her cleaned up and got her a new plate of food. While she appeared a bit shaken up, Ingrid went about enjoying herself the rest of the evening. Ingrid's husband called later telling everyone that his wife had been taken to the hospital—(at 6:00 p.m., Ingrid passed away.) She had suffered a stroke at the BBQ. Had they known how to identify the signs of a stroke, perhaps Ingrid would be with us today. Some don't die. They end up in a helpless, hopeless condition instead. It only takes a minute to read this—a neurologist says that if he can get to a stroke victim within three hours, he can totally reverse the effects of a stroke—totally. He said the trick was getting a stroke recognized, diagnosed, and then getting the patient medically cared for within three hours, which is tough.

Recognizing a Stroke

Thank God for the sense to remember the three steps, STR. Read and Learn! Sometimes symptoms of a stroke are difficult to identify. Unfortunately, the lack of awareness spells disaster. The stroke victim may suffer severe brain damage when people nearby fail to recognize the symptoms of a stroke. Now doctors say a bystander can recognize a stroke by asking three simple questions:

S *Ask the individual to *smile*.

T *Ask the person to *talk*, to speak a simple sentence (Coherently) (i.e., It is sunny out today)

R *Ask him or her to raise both arms.

{Note: Another sign of a stroke is this: Ask the person to "stick" out his tongue. If the tongue is crooked, if it goes to one side or the other that is also an indication of a stroke}

If he or she has trouble with *any one* of these tasks, call 9-1-1 immediately and describe the symptoms to the dispatcher.

ABOUT FAITH

ANDY ROONEY AND PRAYER

Andy Rooney says:

I don't believe in Santa Claus, but I'm not going to sue somebody for singing a Ho-Ho-Ho song in December. I don't agree with Darwin, but I didn't go out and hire a lawyer when my high school teacher taught his Theory of Evolution.

Life, liberty, or your pursuit of happiness will not be endangered because someone says a thirty-second prayer before a football game. So what's the big deal? It's not like somebody is up there reading the entire book of Acts. They're just talking to a

God they believe in and asking him to grant safety to the players on the field and the fans going home from the game.

But it's a Christian prayer, some will argue.

Yes, and this is the United States of America, a country founded on Christian principles. According to our very own phone book, Christian churches outnumber all others better than 200—to—1. So what would you expect—somebody chanting Hare Krishna?

If I went to a football game in Jerusalem, I would expect to hear a Jewish prayer.

If I went to a soccer game in Baghdad, I would expect to hear a Muslim prayer.

If I went to a ping pong match in China, I would expect to hear someone pray to Buddha . . .

And I wouldn't be offended. It wouldn't bother me one bit.

When in Rome . . .

"But what about the atheists?" is another argument?

What about them? Nobody is asking them to be baptized. We're not going to pass the collection plate. Just humor us for thirty seconds. If that's asking too much, bring a walkman or a pair of earplugs. Go to the bathroom. Visit the concession stand. Call your lawyer!

Unfortunately, one or two will make that call. One or two will tell thousands what they can and cannot do. I don't think a short prayer at a football game is going to shake the world's foundations.

Christians are just sick and tired of turning the other cheek while our courts strip us of all our rights. Our parents and grandparents taught us to pray before eating, to pray before we go to sleep. Our Bible tells us to pray without ceasing. Now a handful of people and their lawyers are telling us to cease praying.

God, help us. And if that last sentence offends you, well, just sue me.

The silent majority has been silent too long. It's time we tell that one or two who scream loud enough to be heard that the vast majority doesn't care what they want. It is time that the majority rules!

It's time we tell them, you don't *have* to pray; you don't *have* to say the Pledge of Allegiance; you don't *have* to believe in God or attend services that honor Him. That is *your right*, and we will honor *your right*; but by golly, you are no longer going to take our rights away. We are fighting back, and we *will win*!

Romeo Gacad / AFP

God bless us one and all. Especially those who denounce Him, God bless America, despite all her faults. She is still the greatest nation of all. God bless our service men that are fighting to protect our right to pray and worship God.

Let's make 2009 the year, when the silent majority is heard, and we put God back as the foundation of our families and institutions. And our military forces come home from all the wars.

Keep looking up.

CALLER ID

On a Saturday night several weeks ago, this pastor was working late, and decided to call his wife before he left for home. It was about 10:00 p.m., but his wife didn't answer the phone.

The pastor let the phone ring many times. He thought it was odd that she didn't answer, but decided to wrap up a few things and try again in a few minutes. When he tried again, she answered right away. He asked her why she hadn't answered before, and she said that it hadn't rung at their house. They brushed it off as a fluke and went on their merry ways.

The following Monday, the pastor received a call at the church office, which was the phone that he'd used that Saturday night. The man that he spoke with wanted to know why he'd called on Saturday night.

The pastor couldn't figure out what the man was talking about. Then the man said, "It rang and rang, but I didn't answer." The pastor remembered the mishap and apologized for disturbing him, explaining that he'd intended to call his wife.

The man said, "That's, okay. Let me tell you my story."

You see, I was planning to commit suicide on Saturday night, but before I did, I prayed, "God if you're there, and you don't want me to do this, give me a sign now." At that point my phone started to ring. I looked at the caller ID, and it said, "Almighty God." I was afraid to answer!

The reason why it showed on the man's caller ID that the call came from "Almighty God" is because the church that the pastor attends is called Almighty God Tabernacle!

FLORIDA COURT SETS ATHEIST HOLY DAY

In Florida, an Atheist created a case against the upcoming Easter and Passover holy days. He hired an attorney to bring a discrimination case against Christians and Jews and observances of their holy days. The argument was that it was unfair that atheists had no such recognized days.

The case was brought before a judge. After listening to the passionate presentation by the lawyer, the judge banged his gavel declaring, "Case dismissed!"

The lawyer immediately stood objecting to the ruling saying, "Your honor, how can you possibly dismiss this case? The Christians have Christmas, Easter, and others. The Jews have Passover, Yom Kippur and Hanukkah, yet my client and all other atheists have no such holidays."

The judge leaned forward in his chair saying, "But you do. Your client, counsel, is woefully ignorant." The lawyer said, "Your Honor, we are unaware of any special observance or holiday for atheists."

The judge said, "The calendar says April 1 is April Fools Day. *Psalm 14:1 states, 'The fool says in his heart, there is no God.'* Thus, it is the opinion of this court, that if your client says there is no God, then he is a fool. Therefore, April 1 is his day. Court is adjourned."

You gotta love a Judge that knows his scripture!

FOUR BOYFRIENDS

This turned out to be so different from what I thought it was going to be . . .

It is a wonderful message and if you think it has something to do with "real boyfriends" you will be surprised at the end . . . enjoy.

Once upon a time, there was a girl who had four boyfriends.

She loved the fourth boyfriend the most, and adorned him with rich robes, and treated him to the finest of delicacies. She gave him nothing but the best.

She also loved the third boyfriend very much and was always showing him off to neighboring kingdoms. However, she feared that one day he would leave her for another.

She also loved her second boyfriend. He was her confidant and was always kind, considerate, and patient with her. Whenever this girl faced a problem, she could confide in him, and he would help her get through the difficult times.

The girl's first boyfriend was a very loyal partner and had made great contributions in maintaining her wealth and kingdom. However, she did not love the first boyfriend. Although he loved her deeply, she hardly took notice of him!

One day, the girl fell ill, and she knew her time was short. She thought of her luxurious life and wondered, "I now have four boyfriends with me, but when I die, I'll be all alone . . ."

Thus, she asked the fourth boyfriend, "I loved you the most, endowed you with the finest clothing and showered great care over you. Now that I'm dying, will you follow me and keep me company?"

"No way!" replied the fourth boyfriend, and he walked away without another word. His answer cut like a sharp knife right into her heart.

The sad girl then asked the third boyfriend, "I loved you all my life. Now that I'm dying, will you follow me and keep me company?"

"No!" replied the third boyfriend. "Life is too good! When you die, I'm going to marry someone else!" Her heart sank and turned cold.

She then asked the second boyfriend, "I have always turned to you for help and you've always been there for me. When I die, will you follow me and keep me company?"

"I'm sorry, I can't help you out this time," replied the second boyfriend. "At the very most, I can only walk with you to your grave."

His answer struck her like a bolt of lightning, and the girl was devastated.

Then a voice called out: "I'll go with you. I'll follow you no matter where you go." The girl looked up, and there was her first boyfriend. He was very skinny as he had suffered from malnutrition and neglect.

Greatly grieved, the girl said, "I should have taken much better care of you when I had the chance!"
In truth, you have four boyfriends in your lives:

Your fourth boyfriend is your body. No matter how much time and effort you lavish in making it look good, it will leave you when you die.

Your third boyfriend is your status, wealth, and possessions. When you die, it will all go to others.

Your second boyfriend is your family and friends. No matter how much they have been there for you, the furthest they can stay by you is up to the grave.

And your first boyfriend is your spirit, often neglected in pursuit of wealth, power, and pleasures of the world.

However, your spirit is the only thing that will follow you wherever you go. Cultivate, strengthen, and cherish it now, for it is the only part of you that will follow you to the throne of God and continue with you throughout eternity.

Thought for the day:

Remember, when the world pushes you to your knees, you're in the perfect position to pray.

Pass this on to someone you care about—I just did.

Being happy doesn't mean everything's perfect. It means you've decided to see beyond the imperfections.

MATTHEW 10:32

No one falls in love by choice; it is by *chance*.
No one stays in love by chance; it is by *work*.
And no one falls out of love by chance; it is by *choice*.

He did something for you, now do something for Him. Spread His word, and you'll be rewarded.

Matthew 10:32—"Whoever acknowledges Me before men, I will acknowledge him before My Father in heaven.

But whoever disowns Me before men, I will disown him before My Father in heaven."

ONE SOLITARY LIFE

He was born in an obscure village, a child of a peasant woman.

He grew up in still another obscure village where he worked in a carpenter's shop till he was thirty. And then for three years he was an itinerant preacher.

He never wrote a book.

He never held an office.

He never had a family.

He never owned a house.

He never went to college.

He never visited a big city; He never traveled two hundred miles from the place where he was born.

He did none of those things one usually associates with greatness.

He had no credentials but himself.

He was only thirty-three when the tide of popular opinion turned against him.

His friends ran away.

He was turned over to his enemies and he went through the mockery of a trial.

He was nailed upon a cross between two thieves.

While He was dying, His executioners gambled for his clothing, the only property He had on earth.

When He was dead, He was laid in a borrowed grave through the pity of a friend.

Twenty centuries have come and gone, and today Jesus is the central figure of the human race, the leader of mankind's progress.

All the armies that ever marched, all the navies that have ever sailed, all the parliaments that have ever sat, all the kings that have ever reigned put together, have not affected the life of mankind on this earth as much as that—*One solitary life.*

THE CROSSWALK

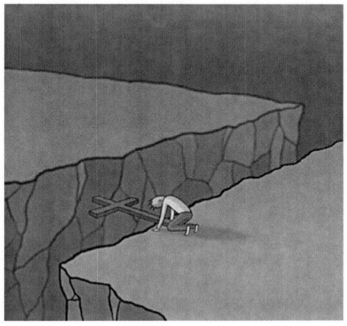

We complain about the cross we bear but don't realize it is preparing us for the dip in the road that God can see and we cannot.

Whatever your cross,
Whatever your pain,
There will always be sunshine, after the rain.
Perhaps you may stumble, perhaps even fall;
But God's always ready, to answer your call.
He knows every heartache, sees every tear,
A word from His lips, can calm every fear.
Your sorrows may linger, throughout the night,
But suddenly vanish, by dawn's early light.
The Savior is waiting, somewhere above, To give you His grace, and send you His love.
May God fill your day with blessings!

Be kinder than necessary, for everyone you meet is fighting some kind of battle!

THE (SCIENTIFIC) DEATH OF JESUS

At the age of thirty-three, Jesus was condemned to death.

That was then the "worst" death. Only the worst criminals could die like Jesus. And with Jesus, things were worse, because not all the criminals condemned to death could receive nails on their hands and feet.

Of course, nails—Big nails! Each was fifteen to twenty cm long, with a point of six cm. Another point was sharp.

The nails were carved into the pulses, and not into the palms, as we are used to hearing. In the pulse, there's a tendon which extends to the shoulder, and when the nails were being hammered, that tendon broke, obliging Jesus to reinforce all the muscles of his back, so that He could breathe as He was losing all the air from His lungs.

In this way, He was forced to support Himself onto the nail carved in His feet, which was bigger than those carved into His pulses, for both feet were carved together. And, as His feet could not endure for long time without tearing, Jesus was forced to alternate that "cycle" so that He could breathe.

Jesus endured that reality for over three hours.

Yes, over three hours! Long time, isn't it? Few minutes before He died, Jesus was not bleeding anymore.
He was simply pouring water from his cuts and holes.

When we imagine Him injured, we only picture Him with injuries, but it is not enough; His wounds were true holes, made in His body.

He had no more blood to bleed, He only poured water.

Human body is composed of nearly 3.5 litres of blood (for adult).

Jesus poured all 3.5 litres of his blood; He had three nails hammered into His members; a crown of thorns on His head and, beyond that, a Roman soldier who nailed a spear into His chest.

All these without mentioning the humiliation, He passed after carrying His own cross for almost two kilometres, while the crowd spat on His face and threw stones (the cross was almost 30 kg of weight, only for its higher part, where His hands were nailed).

He died for us.

He died for you. Accept the reality, the truth that *Jesus is the only salvation for the world.*

God has plans for you.

Without Him, I am nothing, but with Him, "I can do all things through Christ which strengtheneth me" (Phil. 4:13)

THE FOUR CANDLES

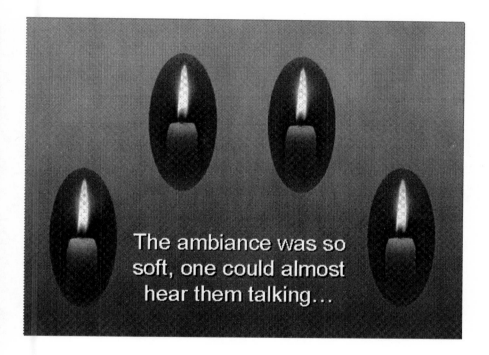

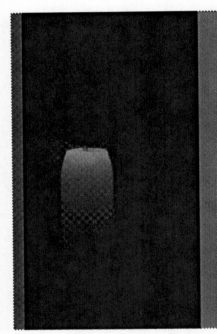

The first candle
said:

"I am Peace!"

"The world is full of anger
and fighting. Nobody can
keep me lit."

Then the flame of Peace
went out completely.

The second candle said:

"I am Faith!"

"I am no longer indispensable. It doesn't make sense that I stay lit another moment."

Just then a breeze softly blew Faith's flame.

Sadly the third candle
began to speak:

"I am Love!"

"People don't understand
my importance so they
simply put me aside. They
even forget to love those
who are nearest to them."

And waiting no longer Love's
flame went out.

Suddenly...

a child entered
the room and saw
the three unlit
candles.

"Why aren't you
burning? You're
supposed to stay
lit till the end."

Saying this, the child began to cry.

The Greatest Of These Is Love...

... but the flame of Hope should never go out of your life!

With hope each of us can live with Peace, Faith and Love.

PRAYER:

"Dear God, You are my light and salvation. You are my hope. Please come into my heart, forgive all my wrongs and give me Your wonderful gift of eternal Life. Help me be an instrument of Your love and cause Your light to shine on others through me. Amen"

THE HOLY ALPHABET

This is truly *beautiful*!

Whoever wrote this must have had some Divine guidance!

A lthough things are not perfect
B ecause of trial or pain
C ontinue in thanksgiving
D o not begin to blame
E ven when the times are hard
F ierce winds are bound to blow
G od is forever able
H old on to what you know
I magine life without His love
J oy would cease to be
K eep thanking Him for all the things
L ove imparts to thee
M ove out of "Camp Complaining"
N o weapon that is known
O n earth can yield the power
P raise can do alone
Q uit looking at the future
R edeem the time at hand
S tart every day with worship
T o "thank" is a command
U ntil we see Him coming
V ictorious in the sky
W e'll run the race with gratitude
X alting God most high

Y es, there'll be good times and yes, some will be bad, but . . .
Z ion awaits us in glory . . . where none are ever sad!

Remember:

The shortest distance between a problem and its solution is the distance between your knees and the floor.

The one who kneels before the Lord can stand up to anything.

The Little Things

As you might remember, the head of a company survived 9/11 *because his son started kindergarten.*

Another fellow was alive because it was *his turn to bring donuts.*

One woman was late because her *alarm clock didn't go off in time.*

One was late because of being stuck on the NJ Turnpike *because of an auto accident.*

One of them *missed his bus.*

One spilled food on her clothes and had to take *time to change.*

One's *car wouldn't start.*

One couldn't *get a taxi.*

The one that struck me was the man, who put on a new pair of shoes that morning, took the various means to get to work but before he got there, he developed a blister on his foot.

He stopped at a drugstore to buy a Band-Aid. That is why he is alive today.

Now when I am stuck in traffic, miss an elevator, turn back to answer a ringing telephone . . . all the little things that annoy me. I think to myself, this is exactly where God wants me to be at this very moment.

Next time your morning seems to be going wrong, the children are slow getting dressed, you can't seem to find the car keys, you hit every traffic light, don't get mad or frustrated;

It may be just that God is at work watching over you.

THE ROSARY

Jim Castle was tired when he boarded his plane in Cincinnati, Ohio, that night in 1981. The forty-five-year-old management consultant had put on a weeklong series of business meetings and seminars, and now he sank gratefully into his seat ready for the flight home to Kansas City, Kansas. As more passengers entered, the place hummed with conversation, mixed with the sound of bags being stowed. Then, suddenly, people fell silent. The quiet moved slowly up the aisle like an invisible wake behind a boat. Jim craned his head to see what was happening, and his mouth dropped open. Walking up the aisle were two nuns clad in simple white habits bordered in blue.

He recognized the familiar face of one at once, the wrinkled skin, and the eyes warmly intent. This was a face he'd seen in newscasts and on the cover of *Time*. The two nuns halted, and Jim realized that his seat companion was going to be Mother Teresa! As the last few passengers settled in, Mother Teresa and her companion pulled out rosaries. Each decade of the beads was a different color, Jim noticed. The decades represented various areas of the world, Mother Teresa told him later, and added, "I pray for the poor and dying on each continent." The airplane taxied to the runway and the two women began to pray, their voices a low murmur. Though Jim considered himself not a very religious Catholic who went to church mostly out of habit, inexplicably he found himself joining in. By the time they murmured the final prayer, the plane had reached cruising altitude.

Mother Teresa turned toward him. For the first time in his life, Jim understood what people meant when they spoke of a person possessing an aura. As she gazed at him, a sense of peace filled him; he could no more see it than he could see the wind but he felt it, just as surely as he felt a warm summer breeze. "Young man," she inquired, "do you say the rosary often?" "No, not really," he admitted. She took his hand, while her eyes probed his. Then she smiled. "Well, you will now." And she dropped her rosary into his palm. An hour later, Jim entered the Kansas City airport where he was met by his wife, Ruth. "What in the world?" Ruth asked when she noticed the rosary in his hand. They kissed and Jim described his encounter.

Driving home, he said. "I feel as if I met a true sister of God." Nine months later Jim and Ruth visited Connie, a friend of theirs for several years. Connie confessed that she'd been told she had ovarian cancer. "The doctor says it's a tough case," said Connie, "but I'm going to fight it. I won't give up." Jim clasped her hand. Then, after reaching into his pocket, he gently twined Mother Teresa's rosary around her fingers. He told her the story and said, "Keep it with you Connie. It may help." Although Connie wasn't Catholic, her hand closed willingly around the small plastic beads. "Thank you," she whispered. "I hope I can return it." More than a year passed before Jim saw Connie again. This time her face was glowing, she hurried toward him and handed him the rosary. "I carried it with me all year," she said. "I've had surgery and have been on chemotherapy, too. Last month, the doctors did second-look surgery, and the tumor's gone, completely!"

Her eyes met Jim's. "I knew it was time to give the rosary back." In the fall of 1987, Ruth's sister, Liz, fell into a deep depression after her divorce. She asked Jim if she could borrow the rosary, and when he sent it, she hung it over her bedpost in a small velvet bag. At night I held on to it, just physically held on. "I was so lonely and afraid," she says, "yet when I gripped that rosary, I felt as if I held a loving hand." Gradually, Liz pulled her life together, and she mailed the rosary back. "Someone else may need it," she said. Then one night in 1988, a stranger telephoned Ruth. She'd heard about the rosary from a neighbor and asked if she could borrow it to take to the hospital where her mother lay in a coma. The family hoped the rosary might help their mother die peacefully. A few days later, the woman returned the beads. "The nurses told me a coma patient can still hear," she said, "so I explained to my mother that I had Mother Teresa's rosary and that when I gave it to her she could let go; it would be all rosary in her hand. Right away, we saw her face relax. The lines smoothed out until she looked so peaceful, so young." The woman's voice caught. "A few minutes later she was gone." Fervently, she gripped Ruth's hands. "Thank you."

Is there special power in those humble beads? Or is the power of the human spirit simply renewed in each person who borrows the rosary? Jim always responds though, whenever he lends the rosary, "When you're through needing it, send it back. Someone else may need it." Jim's own life has changed, too, since his unexpected meeting on the airplane. When he realized Mother Teresa carries everything she owns in a small bag, he made an effort to simplify his own life. "I try to remember what really counts—not money or titles or possessions, but the way we love others," he says.

May god bless you abundantly, may Mother Mary ask her son Jesus to shower you with graces.

ABOUT FAMILY

Taken Away

I was walking around in a Target store, when I saw a cashier hand this little boy some money back.

The boy couldn't have been more than five or six years old.

The cashier said, "I'm sorry, but you don't have enough money to buy this doll."

Then the little boy turned to the old woman next to him: "Granny, are you sure I don't have enough money?"
The old lady replied: "You know that you don't have enough money to buy this doll, my dear."
Then she asked him to stay there for just five minutes while she went to look around. She left quickly.

The little boy was still holding the doll in his hand.

Finally, I walked toward him and I asked him who he wished to give this doll to.

"It's the doll that my sister loved most and wanted so much for Christmas. She was sure that Santa Claus would bring it to her."

I replied to him that maybe Santa Claus would bring it to her after all, and not to worry.

But he replied to me sadly. "No, Santa Claus can't bring it to her where she is now. I have to give the doll to my mommy so that she can give it to my sister when she goes there."

His eyes were so sad while saying this. "My Sister has gone to be with God. Daddy says that Mommy is going to see God very soon too, so I thought that she could take the doll with her to give it to my sister."

My heart nearly stopped . . .

The little boy looked up at me and said: "I told Daddy to tell Mommy not to go yet. I need her to wait until I come back from the mall."

Then he showed me a very nice photo of himself. He was laughing. He then told me "I want Mommy to take my picture with her so she won't forget me."

"I love my mommy, and I wish she didn't have to leave me, but daddy says that she has to go to be with my little sister."

Then he looked again at the doll with sad eyes, very quietly.

I quickly reached for my wallet and said to the boy. "Suppose we check again, just in case you do have enough money for the doll!"

"Okay," he said, "I hope I do have enough." I added some of my money to his without him seeing and we started to count it. There was enough for the doll and even some spare money.

The little boy said, "Thank you God for giving me enough money!"

Then he looked at me and added, "I asked last night before I went to sleep for God to make sure I had enough money to buy this doll, so that mommy could give it to my sister. He heard me!"

"I also wanted to have enough money to buy a white rose for my mommy, but I didn't dare to ask God for too much. But He gave me enough to buy the doll and a white rose."

"My mommy loves white roses."

A few minutes later, the old lady returned, and I left with my basket.

I finished my shopping in a totally different state of mind from when I started. I couldn't get the little boy out of my mind.

Then I remembered a local newspaper article two days ago, which mentioned a drunk man in a truck, who hit a car occupied by a young woman and a little girl. The little girl died right away, and the mother was left in a critical state. The family had to decide whether to pull the plug on the life-sustaining machine, because the young woman would not be able to recover from the coma.

Was this the family of the little boy?

Two days after this encounter with the little boy, I read in the newspaper that the young woman had passed away.

I couldn't stop myself as I bought a bunch of white roses, and I went to the funeral home where the body of the young woman was for people to see and make last wishes before her burial.

She was there, in her coffin, holding a beautiful white rose in her hand with the photo of the little boy and the doll placed over her chest.

I left the place, teary-eyed, feeling that my life had been changed forever. The love that the little boy had for his mother and his sister is still, to this day, hard to imagine.

And in a fraction of a second, a drunk driver had taken all this away from him.

The Fifth Commandment

A Commandment with a Promise

"Honor thy father and thy mother: that thy days may be long upon the land which the LORD thy God giveth thee" (Exod. 20:12)

"Honor thy father and thy mother, as the LORD thy God hath commanded thee; that thy days may be prolonged, and that it may go well with thee, in the land which the LORD thy God giveth thee" (Deut. 5:16)

"Ye shall fear every man his mother and his father . . ." (Lev. 19:3)

"Children, obey your parents in the Lord: for this is right. Honor thy father and thy mother; which is the first commandment with promise; that it may be well with thee, and thou mayest live long on the earth. And, ye fathers provoke not your children to wrath: but bring them up in the nurture and admonition of the Lord," (Eph. 6:1-4)

"Children, obey your parents in all things: for this is well pleasing unto the Lord. Fathers, provoke not your children to anger, lest they be discouraged," (Col. 3:20-21)

"My son, hear the instruction of thy father, and forsake not the law of thy mother," (Prov. 1:8)

"A wise son maketh a glad father: but a foolish man despiseth his mother," (Prov. 15:20)

"Children are the crown of old men; and the glory of children are their fathers," and, "A foolish son is a grief to his father, and bitterness to her that bare him," (Prov. 17:6, 25)

"A foolish son is the calamity of his father," and, "He that wasteth his father, and chaseth away his mother, is a son that causeth shame, and bringeth reproach," (Prov. 19:13, 26)

"Hearken unto thy father that begat thee, and despise not thy mother when she is old," (Prov. 23:22)

"Correct thy son, and he shall give thee rest; yea, he shall give delight unto thy soul," (Prov. 29:17)

"For whom the Lord loveth He chasteneth, and scourgeth every son whom He receiveth," (Heb. 12:6)

THE WOODEN BOWL

I guarantee you will remember the tale of the Wooden Bowl tomorrow, a week from now, a month from now, a year from now.

A frail old man went to live with his son, daughter-in-law, and four-year-old grandson. The old man's hands trembled, his eyesight was blurred, and his step faltered.

The family ate together at the table. But the elderly grandfather's shaky hands and failing sight made eating difficult. Peas rolled off his spoon onto the floor. When he grasped the glass, milk spilled on the tablecloth.

The son and daughter-in-law became irritated with the mess. "We must do something about father," said the son. "I've had enough of his spilled milk, noisy eating, and food on the floor."

So the husband and wife set a small table in the corner. There, Grandfather ate alone while the rest of the family enjoyed dinner. Since Grandfather had broken a dish or two, his food was served in a wooden bowl.

When the family glanced in Grandfather's direction, sometimes he had a tear in his eye as he sat alone. Still, the only words the couple had for him were sharp admonitions when he dropped a fork or spilled food.

The four-year-old watched it all in silence.

One evening before supper, the father noticed his son playing with wood scraps on the floor.

He asked the child sweetly, "What are you making?" Just as sweetly, the boy responded, "Oh, I am making a little bowl for you and Mama to eat your food in when I grow up." The four-year-old smiled and went back to work.

The words so struck the parents so that they were speechless. Then tears started to stream down their cheeks. Though no word was spoken, both knew what must be done.

That evening the husband took Grandfather's hand and gently led him back to the family table. For the remainder of his days, he ate every meal with the family. And for some reason, neither the husband nor the wife seemed to care any longer when a fork was dropped, milk spilled, or the tablecloth soiled.

~ ~ ~ ~ ~ ~ ~ ~ ~ ~ ~

On a positive note, I've learned that, no matter what happens, how bad it seems today, life does go on, and it will be better tomorrow.

I've learned that you can tell a lot about a person by the way he/she handles four things: a rainy day, the elderly, lost luggage, and tangled Christmas tree lights.

I've learned that making a living is not the same thing as making a life . . .

I've learned that life sometimes gives you a second chance.

I've learned that you shouldn't go through life with a catcher's mitt on both hands. You need to be able to throw something back sometimes.

I've learned that if you pursue happiness, it will elude you. But, if you focus on your family, your friends, the needs of others, your work and doing the very best you can, happiness will find you.

I've learned that whenever I decide something with an open heart, I usually make the right decision.

I've learned that even when I have pains, I don't have to be one.

I've learned that every day, you should reach out and touch someone.

People love that human touch—holding hands, a warm hug, or just a friendly pat on the back.

I've learned that I still have a lot to learn.

WOMEN'S FAVORITE E-MAIL

A man was sick and tired of going to work every day while his wife stayed home. He wanted her to see what he went through, so he prayed:

> "Dear Lord: I go to work every day and put in eight hours while my wife merely stays at home. I want her to know what I go through. So, please allow her body to switch with mine for a day."'

God, in his infinite wisdom, granted the man's wish.

The next morning, sure enough, the man awoke as a woman. He arose, cooked breakfast for his mate, awakened the kids, set out their school clothes, fed them breakfast, packed their lunches, drove them to school, came home and picked up the dry cleaning, took it to the cleaners and stopped at the bank to make a deposit, went grocery shopping, then drove home to put away the groceries, paid the bills and balanced the check book. He cleaned the cat's litter box and bathed the dog.

Then, it was already 1:00 p.m. And he hurried to make the beds, do the laundry, vacuum, dust and sweep and mop the kitchen floor, ran to the school to pick up the kids and got into an argument with them on the way home, set out milk and cookies and got the kids organized to do their homework, then, set up the ironing board and watched TV while he did the ironing.

At 4:30 p.m., he began peeling potatoes and washing vegetables for salad, breaded the pork chops and snapped fresh beans for supper.

After supper, he cleaned the kitchen, ran the dishwasher, folded laundry, bathed the kids, and put them to bed.

At 9:00 p.m., he was exhausted and, though his daily chores weren't finished, he went to bed where he was expected to make love, which he managed to get through without complaint.

The next morning, he awoke and immediately knelt by the bed and said:

> *"Lord, I don't know what I was thinking. I was so wrong to envy my wife's being able to stay home all day.*
> *Please, Oh! Please, let us trade back. Amen!"*

The Lord, in his infinite wisdom, replied:

"My son, I feel you have learned your lesson, and I will be happy to change things back to the way they were. You'll just have to wait nine months, though. You got pregnant last night."

ABOUT HEALTH

Advice for Diabetics

Some newly discovered compounds have just been found to turn off all of the genes that cause diabetes.

Are these compounds found in a pill bottle?

No way.

Instead, you'll find them on your dinner plate—in rye bread and pasta. (As I recently wrote in one of my blogs, rye contains special phytonutrients that turn off all the genes responsible for diabetes in just a few weeks.)

Last week, I explained how to find out if you are prediabetic or diabetic. Half of people with diabetes don't know they have it and nearly all the people with prediabetes don't know they have it.

Today, I want to share with you more information about what you can do *now* to prevent and reverse diabetes and prediabetes.

And rye bread isn't the only answer. I've got a lot more good advice, too.

Let's get started.

Dietary Recommendations

Eating in a way that balances your blood sugar, reduces inflammation and oxidative stress, and improves your liver detoxification is the key to preventing and reversing insulin resistance and diabetes.

This is a way of eating that is based on a whole foods diet that's high in fiber, rich in colorful fruits and vegetables, and low in sugars and flours, with a low glycemic load.

It is a way of eating that includes anti-inflammatory, antioxidant, and detoxifying foods. It includes plenty of omega-3 fats and olive oil, soy products, beans, nuts, and seeds.

All these foods help prevent and reverse diabetes and insulin resistance. This is the way of eating that turns on all the right gene messages, promotes a healthy metabolism, and prevents aging and age related diseases like diabetes and heart disease.

Here are more specifics.

Meal Timing

- Eat protein for breakfast every day, such as whole omega-3 eggs, a soy protein shake, or nut butters.

- Eat something every four hours to keep your insulin and glucose levels normal.

- Eat small protein snacks in the morning and afternoon, such as a handful of almonds.

- Finish eating at least two to three hours before bed. If you have a snack earlier in the day, you won't be as hungry, even if you eat a little later.

Meal Composition

- Controlling the glycemic load of your meals is very important.

- You can do this by combining adequate protein, fats, and whole-food carbohydrates from vegetables, legumes, nuts, seeds, and fruit at every meal or snack.

- It is most important to avoid eating quickly absorbed carbohydrates alone, as they raise your sugar and insulin levels.

Travel Suggestions

Two handfuls of almonds in a ziplock bag make a useful emergency snack. You can eat them with a piece of fruit. Remember, real food is the best.

Choose from a variety of the following real, whole foods:

- Choose organic produce and animal products whenever possible.

- Eat high-quality protein, such as fish—especially fatty, coldwater fish like salmon, sable, small halibut, herring, sardines, and shellfish.

- Coldwater fish such as salmon, halibut, and sable contain an abundance of beneficial essential fatty acids, omega-3 oils that reduce inflammation. Smaller wild Alaskan salmon, sable, and halibut that are low in toxins. Canned wild salmon is a great emergency food.

- Eat up to eight omega-3 eggs a week.

- Create meals that are high in low-glycemic legumes such as lentils, chickpeas, and soybeans (try edamame, the Japanese soybeans in a pod, quickly steamed with a little salt, as a snack). These foods slow the release of sugars into the bloodstream, which helps prevent the excess insulin release that can lead to health concerns like obesity, high blood pressure, and heart problems.

- Eat a cornucopia of fresh fruits and vegetables teeming with phytonutrients like carotenoids, flavonoids, and polyphenols, which are associated with a lower incidence of nearly all health problems, including obesity and age-related disease.

- Eat more low-glycemic vegetables, such as asparagus, broccoli, kale, spinach, cabbage, and brussels sprouts.

- Berries, cherries, peaches, plums, rhubarb, pears, and apples are optimal fruits. Cantaloupes and other melons, grapes, and kiwifruit are suitable; however, they contain more sugar. You can use organic frozen berries (such as those from Cascadian Farms) in your protein shakes.

- Focus on anti-inflammatory foods, including wild fish and other sources of omega-3 fats, red and purple berries (these are rich in polyphenols), dark green leafy vegetables, orange, sweet potatoes, and nuts.

- Eat more antioxidant-rich foods, including orange and yellow vegetables, dark green leafy vegetables (kale, collards, spinach, etc.), anthocyanidins (berries, beets, grapes, pomegranate), purple grapes, blueberries, bilberries, cranberries, and cherries. In fact, antioxidants are in all colorful fruits and vegetables.

- Include detoxifying foods in your diet, such as cruciferous vegetables (broccoli, kale, collards, brussels sprouts, cauliflower, bokchoy, chinese cabbage, and chinese broccoli), green tea, watercress, dandelion greens, cilantro, artichokes, garlic, citrus peels, pomegranate, and even cocoa.

- Season your food with herbs such as rosemary, ginger, and turmeric, which are powerful antioxidants, anti-inflammatory agents, and detoxifiers.

- Avoid excessive quantities of meat. Eat lean organic or grass-fed animal products, when possible. These include eggs, beef, chicken, pork, lamb, buffalo, and ostrich. There are good brands at Whole Foods and other local health-food stores (also see mail order sources).

- Garlic and onions contain antioxidants, enhance detoxification, act as anti-inflammatory agents, and help lower cholesterol and blood pressure.

- A diet high in fiber further helps to stabilize blood sugar by slowing the absorption of carbohydrates and supports a healthy lower bowel and digestive tract. Try to gradually increase fiber to thirty to fifty grams a day and use predominantly soluble or viscous fiber (legumes, nuts, seeds, whole grains, vegetables, and fruit), which slows sugar absorption from the gut.

- Use extra virgin olive oil, which contains anti-inflammatory and anti-oxidant properties, as your main cooking oil.

- Soy products such as soymilk, soybeans, and tofu are rich in antioxidants that can reduce cancer risk, lower cholesterol, and improve insulin and blood sugar metabolism.

- Increase your intake of nuts and seeds, including raw walnuts, almonds, macadamia nuts, and pumpkin and flax seeds.

- And yes, chocolate can be healthy, too. Choose only the darkest varieties and eat only two to three ounces a day. It should contain 70 percent cocoa.

Decrease (or ideally eliminate) your intake of:

- All processed or junk foods.

- Foods containing refined white flour and sugar, such as breads, cereals (cornflakes, Frosted Flakes, puffed wheat, and sweetened granola), flour-based pastas, bagels, and pastries.

- All foods containing high-fructose corn syrup.

- All artificial sweeteners (aspartame, Sorbitol, etc.) and caffeine.

- Starchy, high-glycemic cooked vegetables, such as potatoes, corn, and root vegetables such as rutabagas, parsnips, and turnips.

- Processed fruit juices, which are often loaded with sugars (try juicing your own carrots, celery, and beets, or other fruit and vegetable combinations, instead).

- Processed canned vegetables (usually very high in sodium).

- Foods containing hydrogenated or partially hydrogenated oils (which become trans-fatty acids in the bloodstream), such as most crackers, chips, cakes, candies, cookies, doughnuts, and processed cheese.

- Processed oils such as corn, safflower, sunflower, peanut, and canola.

- Red meats (unless organic or grass-fed) and organ meats.

- Large predatory fish and river fish, which contain mercury and other contaminants in unacceptable amounts, including swordfish, tuna, tilefish, and shark.

- Dairy—substitute unsweetened, gluten free soymilk, almond milk, or hazelnut milk products.

- Alcohol—limit it to no more than three glasses a week of red wine per week.

Exercise

Exercise is critical for the improvement of insulin sensitivity. It helps reduce central body fat, improving sugar metabolism. Regular exercise will help prevent diabetes, reduce your risk of complications, and even help reverse it.

Ideally, you should do thirty minutes of walking every day. Walking after dinner is a powerful way to reduce your blood sugar.

More vigorous exercise and sustained exercise is often needed to reverse severe insulin resistance or diabetes. Doing sustained aerobic exercise for up to sixty minutes, five to six times a week is often necessary to get diabetes under full control. You want to work at 70 to 85 percent of your target heart rate, which you can find by subtracting your age from 220 and multiplying that number by 0.70 to 0.85.

Interval training can be an added benefit to helping improve your metabolism and mitochondrial function. It helps to increase the efficiency calorie burning so that you burn more calories and energy during the time you are *not* exercising. This is described in detail in UltraMetabolism.

Strength training also helps maintain and build muscle, which can help also with your overall blood sugar and energy metabolism.

Supplementation

- Nutritional supplements can be very effective for Type 2 diabetes and insulin resistance. I recommend a number of different supplements, depending on the severity of the problem:

- Multivitamin and mineral.

- Calcium and magnesium and vitamin D.

- Fish oil (1,000 to 4,000 mg) a day improves insulin sensitivity, lowers cholesterol, and reduces inflammation.

- Extra magnesium (200 to 600 mg a day) helps with glucose metabolism and is often deficient in diabetics.

- Chromium (500 to 1,000 mcg a day) is very important for proper sugar metabolism.

- Antioxidants (such as vitamins C and E) are important in helping to reduce and balance blood sugar.

- B-complex vitamins are important and are part of a good multivitamin. Extra vitamin B6 (50 to 150 mg a day) and B12 (1,000 to 3,000 mcg) are especially helpful in protecting against diabetic neuropathy or nerve damage.

- Biotin (2,000 to 4,000 mcg a day) enhances insulin sensitivity.

- I also encourage people to use alpha-lipoic acid (300 mg twice a day), a powerful antioxidant that can reduce blood sugar significantly. It also can be effective for diabetic nerve damage or neuropathy.

- Evening primrose oil (500 to 1,000 mg twice a day) helps overcome deficiencies common in diabetics.

- I encourage people to use cinnamon as a supplement. One to two 500 mg tablets twice a day can help blood sugar control.

- Other herbs and supplements that can be helpful include green tea, ginseng, bitter melon, gymnema, bilberry, ginkgo, onions, and garlic. Fenugreek can also be used to help improve blood sugar, although large amounts must be taken.

- Banaba leaf (Lagerstroemia speciosa) can be an effective herb. Take 24 mg twice a day. I recommend konjac fiber, such as PGX (WellBetX), four capsules ten minutes before meals with a glass of water. This helps reduce blood sugar after meals and improves long-term blood sugar control while reducing appetite and cholesterol.

Stress Management

Stress plays a dramatic role in blood sugar imbalances. It triggers insulin resistance, promotes weight gain around the middle, increases inflammation, and ultimately can cause diabetes. So it's essential to engage in relaxation practices on a regular basis, such as yoga, breathing, progressive muscle relaxation, guided imagery, hot baths, exercise, meditation, massage, biofeedback, hypnosis, or even making love. Your survival depends on it.

Medications

A number of medications may be helpful for diabetes. There are several specific classes of medications, each with their own effects. Sometimes combinations are helpful.

These are the main classes.

- The biguanides, especially metformin (Glucophage), is one of the best medications to improve insulin sensitivity. It can help lower blood sugars by improving your cells' response to insulin.

- Thiazolidinedione drugs are a new class of diabetes medication and can help improve uptake of glucose by the cells by making you more insulin-sensitive. They also reduce inflammation and help improve metabolism working on the PPAR, a special class of cell receptors that control metabolism. They can cause weight gain and liver damage. Thiazolidinediones include rosiglitazone (Avandia) and pioglitazone (Actos).

- Alpha-glucosidase inhibitors include acarbose and miglitol, which can help lower the absorption of sugar and carbohydrates in the intestines, reducing the absorption of sugar after meals.

- Older medications include sulfonylureas include glipizide, glyburide, and glimepiride. I strongly recommend against these medications because they only reduce your sugar in the short term and cause further insulin production, which actually worsens diabetes over the long term. They have also been linked to high risk of heart attacks, which you are trying to prevent. They treat the symptoms rather than the cause.

- Insulin is the last resort after all other measures have failed and often leads to a slippery slope of weight gain and increased cholesterol and blood pressure. Many patients have been able to come off insulin entirely if they are treated early and aggressively through the other methods I've listed.

Summary

Diabetes and its precursor, insulin resistance, are looming as the major threat to our health in the twenty-first century. This is a tragic consequence of our toxic food environment, our unmitigated exposure to stress, and our sedentary lifestyle.

However, these problems are completely preventable and often reversible through aggressive lifestyle changes, supplements, and exercise and stress management.

Diabetes is the biggest health epidemic triggered by the obesity epidemic, but all of our medical efforts to treat it are focused on medications and insulin.

It is simply the wrong approach.

If you follow these guidelines instead, you will see a dramatic change very quickly in your health, your weight, and your diabetes.

Just try it!

For your good health,

Mark Hyman, MD

ASPARAGUS AND CANCER

Several years ago, I had a man seeking asparagus for a friend who had cancer. He gave me a photocopied copy of an article, entitled, "Asparagus for cancer" printed in *Cancer News Journal*, December 1979.

I will share it here, just as it was shared with me: I am a biochemist, and have specialized in the relation of diet to health for over fifty years. Several years ago, I learned of the discovery of Richard R. Vensal, DDS that asparagus might cure cancer.

Since then, I have worked with him on his project. We have accumulated a number of favorable case histories.

Here are a few examples:

Case No. 1: A man with an almost hopeless case of Hodgkin's disease (cancer of the lymph glands) and was completely incapacitated, within one year of starting the asparagus therapy, showed no signs of cancer and was back on a schedule of strenuous exercise.

Case No. 2: A successful businessman, sixty-eight years old suffered from cancer of the bladder for sixteen years.

After years of medical treatments, including radiation, without improvement, he started taking asparagus. Within three months, examinations revealed that his bladder tumor had disappeared and that his kidneys were normal.

Case No. 3: A man who had lung cancer

On March 5, 1971, he was put on the operating table where they found lung cancer so widely spread that it was inoperable. The surgeon sewed him up and declared his case hopeless. On April 5, he heard about the asparagus therapy and immediately started taking it. By August, x-ray pictures revealed that all signs of the cancer had disappeared. He is back at his regular business routine.

Case No. 4: A woman who was troubled for a number of years with skin cancer.

She finally developed different skin cancers, which were diagnosed by asking specialist as advanced. Within three months after starting on asparagus, her skin specialist said that her skin looked fine and no more skin lesions. This woman reported that the asparagus therapy also cured her kidney disease, which started in 1949. She had over ten operations for kidney stones, and was receiving government disability payments for an inoperable, terminal, kidney condition. She attributes the cure of this kidney trouble entirely to the asparagus.

I was not surprised at this result, as "The elements of Materia Medica," edited in 1854, by a professor at the University of Pennsylvania, stated that asparagus was used as a popular remedy for kidney stones. He even referred to experiments, in 1739, on the power of asparagus in dissolving stones.

We would have had other case histories, but the medical establishment has interfered with our obtaining some of the records. I am therefore appealing to readers to spread this good news and help us to gather a large number of case histories that will overwhelm the medical skeptics about this unbelievably simple and natural remedy. For the treatment, asparagus should be cooked before using, and therefore canned asparagus is just as good as fresh.

I have corresponded with the two leading canners of asparagus, Giant Giant and Stokely, and I am satisfied that these brands contain no pesticides or preservatives.

Procedure:

1) Place the cooked asparagus in a blender and liquefy to make a puree, and store in the refrigerator.

2) Give the patient four full tablespoons twice daily, morning and evening.

Patients usually show some improvement in from two to four weeks. It can be diluted with water and used as a cold or hot drink. This suggested dosage is based on present experience, but certainly larger amounts can do no harm and may be needed in some cases.

As a biochemist I am convinced of the old saying that "what cures can prevent." Based on this theory, my wife and I have been using asparagus puree as a beverage with our meals.

We take two tablespoons diluted in water to suit our taste with breakfast and with dinner. I take mine hot and my wife prefers hers cold.

For years, we have made it a practice to have blood surveys taken as part of our regular checkups.

The last blood survey, taken by a medical doctor who specializes in the nutritional approach to health, showed substantial improvements in all categories over the last one, and we can attribute these improvements to nothing but the asparagus drink.

As a biochemist, I have made an extensive study of all aspects of cancer, and all of the proposed cures. As a result, I am convinced that asparagus fits in better with the latest theories about cancer. Asparagus contains a good supply of protein called histones, which are believed to be active in controlling cell growth. For that reason, I believe asparagus can be said to contain a substance that I call cell growth normalizer. That accounts for its action on cancer and in acting as a general body tonic. In any event, regardless of theory, asparagus used as we suggest, is a harmless substance.

The FDA cannot prevent you from using it, and it may do you much good. It has been reported by the U.S. National Cancer Institute, that asparagus is the highest tested food containing glutathione, which is considered one of the body's most potent anticarcinogens and antioxidants.

BANANAS

I am going to eat a banana a day now. After Reading *this*, you'll *never* look at a banana in the same way again.

Bananas—contain three natural sugars—**sucrose, fructose, and glucose** combined with fiber; a banana gives an instant, sustained, and substantial boost of energy. Research has proven that just two bananas provide enough energy for a strenuous ninety-minute workout. No wonder the banana is the number one fruit with the world's leading athletes.

But energy isn't the only way a banana can help us keep fit. It can also help overcome or prevent a substantial number of illnesses and conditions, making it a must to add to our daily diet.

Anemia: High in iron, bananas can stimulate the production of hemoglobin in the blood and so helps in cases of anemia.

Blood Pressure: This unique tropical fruit is extremely high in potassium, yet low in salt, making it the perfect to beat blood pressure. So much so, the U.S. Food and Drug Administration has just allowed the banana industry to make official claims for the fruit's ability to reduce the risk of blood pressure and stroke.

Brain Power: Two hundred students at a Twickenham (Middlesex) school were helped through their exams this year by eating bananas at breakfast, break, and lunch in a bid to boost their brain power. Research has shown that the potassium-packed fruit can assist learning by making pupils more alert.

Constipation: High in fiber, including bananas in the diet can help restore normal bowel action, helping to overcome the problem without resorting to laxatives.

Depression: According to a recent survey undertaken by *mind* amongst people suffering from depression, many felt much better after eating a banana. This is because bananas contain tryptophan, a type of protein that the body converts into serotonin, known to make you relax, improve your mood, and generally make you feel happier.

Hangovers: One of the quickest ways of curing a hangover is to make a banana milkshake, sweetened with honey. The banana calms the stomach and, with the help of the honey, builds up depleted blood sugar levels, while the milk soothes and rehydrates your system.

Heartburn: Bananas have a natural antacid effect in the body, so if you suffer from heartburn, try eating a banana for soothing relief.

Morning Sickness: Snacking on bananas between meals helps to keep blood sugar levels up and avoid morning sickness.

Mosquito bites: Before reaching for the insect bite cream, try rubbing the affected area with the inside of a banana skin. Many people find it amazingly successful at reducing swelling and irritation.

Nerves: Bananas are high in B vitamins that help calm the nervous system. Overweight and at work? Studies at the Institute of Psychology in Austria found pressure at work leads to gorging on comfort food like chocolate and crisps. Looking at five thousand hospital patients, researchers found the most obese were more likely to be in high-pressure jobs. The report concluded that to avoid panic-induced food cravings, we need to control our blood sugar levels by snacking on high carbohydrate foods every two hours to keep levels steady.

PMS: Forget the pills—eat a banana. The vitamin B6 it contains regulates blood glucose levels, which can affect your mood.

Seasonal Affective Disorder (SAD): Bananas can help SAD sufferers because they contain the natural mood enhancer tryptophan.

Smoking: Bananas can also help people trying to give up smoking. The B6, B12 they contain, as well as the potassium and magnesium found in them, help the body recover from the effects of nicotine withdrawal.

Stress: Potassium is a vital mineral, which helps normalize the heartbeat, sends oxygen to the brain and regulates your body's water balance. When we are stressed, our metabolic rate rises, thereby reducing our potassium levels. These can be rebalanced with the help of a high-potassium banana snack.

Strokes: According to research in The New England Journal of Medicine, eating bananas as part of a regular diet can cut the risk of death by strokes by as much as 40 percent!

Temperature control: Many other cultures see bananas as a cooling fruit that can lower both the physical and emotional temperature of expectant mothers. In Thailand, for example, pregnant women eat bananas to ensure their baby is born with a cool temperature.

Ulcers: The banana is used as the dietary food against intestinal disorders because of its soft texture and smoothness. It is the only raw fruit that can be eaten without distress in overchronicler cases. It also neutralizes overacidity and reduces irritation by coating the lining of the stomach.

Warts: Those keen on natural alternatives swear that if you want to kill off a wart, take a piece of banana skin and place it on the wart, with the yellow side out. Carefully hold the skin in place with a plaster or surgical tape!

So, a banana really is a natural remedy for many ills. When you compare it to an apple, it has four times the protein, twice the carbohydrate, three times the phosphorus, five times the vitamin A and iron, and twice the other vitamins and minerals. It is also rich in potassium and is one of the best value foods around. So maybe it's time to change that well-known phrase so that we say, "A banana a day keeps the doctor away!"

PS. Bananas must be the reason monkeys are so happy all the time!

CANCER PREVENTION

Something to think about before your next bite

Here's some very useful and important information about cancer prevention:

1. Every person has cancer cells in the body. These cancer cells do not show up in the standard tests until they have multiplied to a few billion. When doctors tell cancer patients that there are no more cancer cells in their bodies after treatment, it just means the tests are unable to detect the cancer cells because they have not reached the detectable size.

2. Cancer cells occur between six to more than ten times in a person's lifetime.

3. When the person's immune system is strong, the cancer cells will be destroyed and prevented from multiplying and forming tumors.

4. When a person has cancer, it indicates the person has multiple nutritional deficiencies. These could be due to genetic, environmental, food, and lifestyle factors.

5. To overcome the multiple nutritional deficiencies, changing diet and including supplements will strengthen the immune system.

6. Chemotherapy involves poisoning the rapidly-growing cancer cells and also destroys rapidly-growing healthy cells in the bone marrow, gastro-intestinal tract etc, and can cause organ damage, like liver, kidneys, heart, lungs etc.

7. Radiation while destroying cancer cells also burns, scars, and damages healthy cells, tissues, and organs.

8. Initial treatment with chemotherapy and radiation will often reduce tumor size. However, prolonged use of chemotherapy and radiation do not result in more tumor destruction.

9. When the body has too much toxic burden from chemotherapy and radiation, the immune system is either compromised or destroyed, hence the person can succumb to various kinds of infections and complications.

10. Chemotherapy and radiation can cause cancer cells to mutate and become resistant, and difficult to destroy. Surgery can also cause cancer cells to spread to other sites.

11. An effective way to battle cancer is to starve the cancer cells by not feeding it with the foods it needs to multiply.

    *   Sugar is a cancer feeder. By cutting off sugar, it cuts off one important food supply to the cancer cells. Sugar substitutes like NutraSweet, Equal, Spoonful, etc., are made with Aspartame, and it is harmful. A better natural substitute would be Manuka honey or molasses but only in very small amounts.
    *   Milk causes the body to produce mucus, especially in the gastro-intestinal tract. Cancer feeds on mucus. By cutting off milk and substituting with unsweetened soya milk, cancer cells are being starved. Milo, Ovaltine, Horlicks are made with milk and best be avoided.
    *   Cancer cells thrive in an acid environment. A meat-based diet is acidic, and it is best to eat fish, and a little chicken rather than beef or pork. Meat also contains livestock antibiotics, growth hormones, parasites, etc., which are all harmful to people with cancer.
    *   A diet made of 80 percent fresh vegetables and juice, whole grains, seeds, nuts, and a little fruits help put the body into an alkaline environment. About 20 percent can be from cooked food including beans. Fresh vegetable juices provide live enzymes that are easily absorbed and reach down to cellular levels within fifteen minutes to nourish and enhance growth of healthy cells.
    *   Avoid coffee, tea, and chocolate, which have caffeine. Green tea is a better alternative and has cancer-fighting properties.

12. Meat protein is difficult to digest and requires a lot of digestive enzymes. Undigested meat remaining in the intestines become putrefied and leads to more toxic buildup.

13. Cancer cell walls have a tough protein covering. By refraining from or eating less meat it frees more enzymes to attack the protein walls of cancer cells and allows the body's killer cells to destroy the cancer cells.

14. Some supplements build up the immune system (IP6 Flor-ssence, Essiac, antioxidants, vitamins, minerals, EFAs etc.) to enable the body's own killer cells to destroy cancer cells. Other supplements (Maitake for e.g.) are known to cause cancer cells apoptosis, that is, induce cancer cells to commit suicide.

15. Cancer is a disease of the mind, body, and spirit. A proactive and positive spirit will help the cancer warrior be a survivor. Anger, unforgiveness, and bitterness put the body into a stressful and acidic environment. Learn to have a loving and forgiving spirit. Learn to relax, enjoy, and trust God for healing.

16. Cancer cells cannot thrive in an oxygenated environment. Daily exercise and deep breathing help to get more oxygen down to the cellular level. Oxygen therapy is another means employed to destroy cancer cells.

17. Cancer can be reversed with nutrition, supplements, and clinically proven complementary and alternative therapies.

18. Cancer can be healed by the divine intervention of God the Healer.

Summary

1. Sugar is a cancer feeder. Avoid sugar. Sugar substitutes like Equal, Spoonful, NutraSweet are made with aspartame, a chemical that is harmful to the body. A better natural alternative is Manuka honey in small amounts.

2. Milk causes the body to produce mucus. Cancer thrives on mucus. A better calcium alternative is unsweetened soya milk.

3. Green tea has anticancer properties. It is a better substitute for coffee and tea, which have caffeine, bad for people with cancer.

4. Table salt has a chemical added to make it white in color. Better alternative is Bragg's aminos or sea salt.

5. Meat like pork, beef, and chicken contain livestock antibiotics, growth hormones, parasites, etc., which are all harmful for people with cancer. It is

better to eat fish, or eat a little free-range chicken. Meat protein is difficult to digest and requires a lot of digestive enzymes. Undigested meat remaining in the intestines become putrefied and leads to more toxic build up.

6. Cancer cell walls have a tough protein covering. By refraining from or eating less meat, it frees more enzymes to attack the protein walls of cancer cells and allows the body's killer cells to destroy the cancer cells.

7. Water—best to drink purified water, or filtered, to avoid known toxins and heavy metals in tap water. Distilled water is acidic, avoid it.

8. To obtain live enzymes for building healthy cells try and drink fresh vegetable juice (most vegetables including bean sprouts) and eat some raw vegetables two or three times a day. Enzymes are destroyed at temperatures of 104°F (40°C).

A little effort at our part will yield great return in the long run . . . keep up the discipline and enjoy every single moment in life. The point is not to pay back kindness, but to pass it on.

CAR AIR CONDITIONER ALERT

Do not turn on AC immediately as soon as you enter the car! Open the windows after you enter your car and do not turn *on* the air conditioner immediately.

According to a research done, the car dashboard, sofa, air freshener emits Benzene, a cancer-causing toxin (carcinogen—take note of the heated plastic smell in your car).

In addition to causing cancer, it poisons your bones, causes anemia, and reduces white blood cells.

Prolonged exposure will cause leukemia, increasing the risk of cancer. It may also cause miscarriage.

Acceptable Benzene level indoors is 50 mg per sq. ft. A car parked indoors with the windows closed will contain 400—800 mg of Benzene.

If parked outdoors under the sun at a temperature above 60° F, the Benzene level goes up to 2,000—4,000 mg, forty times the acceptable level and the people inside the car will inevitably inhale an excess amount of the toxins.

It is recommended that you open the windows and door to give time for the interior to air out before you enter.

Benzene is a toxin that affects your kidney and liver, and is very difficult for your body to expel this toxic stuff.

Drink Water on Empty Stomach

It is popular in Japan today to drink water immediately after waking up every morning. Furthermore, scientific tests have proven its value. We publish below a description of use of water for our readers. For old and serious diseases as well as modern illnesses the water treatment had been found successful by a Japanese medical society as a 100 percent cure for the following diseases: Headache, body ache, heart system, arthritis, fast heart beat, epilepsy, excess fatness, bronchitis asthma, TB, meningitis, kidney and urine diseases, vomiting, gastritis, diarrhea, piles, diabetes, constipation, all eye diseases, womb, cancer and menstrual disorders, ear, nose, and throat diseases.

Method of Treatment

1. As you wake up in the morning, before brushing teeth, drink 4 × 160 ml glasses of water.
2. Brush and clean the mouth but do not eat or drink anything for forty-five minutes.
3. After forty-five minutes, you may eat and drink as normal.
4. After fifteen minutes of breakfast, lunch, and dinner do not eat or drink anything for two hours.
5. Those that are old or sick and are unable to drink four glasses of water at the beginning may commence by taking little water and gradually increase it to four glasses per day.
6. The above method of treatment will cure diseases of the sick, and others can enjoy a healthy life.

The following list gives the number of days of treatment required to treat main diseases:

1. High Blood Pressure (30 days)
2. Gastric (10 days)
3. Diabetes (30 days)
4. Constipation (10 days)
5. Cancer (180 days)
6. TB (90 days)
7. Arthritis patients should follow the above treatment only for three days in the first week, and from second week onward—daily.

This treatment method has no side effects, however at the commencement of treatment you may have to urinate a few times.

It is better if we continue this and make this procedure as a routine work in our life. Drink water and stay healthy and active.

This makes sense. The Chinese and Japanese drink hot tea with their meals, not cold water. Maybe it is time we adopt their drinking habit while eating! Nothing to lose, everything to gain.

For those who like to drink cold water, this article is applicable to you. It is nice to have a cup of cold drink after a meal. However, the cold water will solidify the oily stuff that you have just consumed. It will slow down the digestion.

Once this sludge reacts with the acid, it will break down and be absorbed by the intestine faster than the solid food. It will line the intestine.

Very soon, this will turn into fats and lead to cancer. It is best to drink hot soup or warm water after a meal.

A serious note about heart attacks:

- Women should know that not every heart attack symptom is going to be the left arm hurting,
- Be aware of intense pain in the jaw line.
- You may never have the first chest pain during the course of a heart attack.
- Nausea and intense sweating are also common symptoms.

- 60 percent of people who have a heart attack while they are asleep do not wake up.
- Pain in the jaw can wake you from a sound sleep. Let's be careful and be aware. The more we know the better chance we could survive.

A cardiologist says if everyone who gets this mail sends it to everyone he knows, you can be sure that we'll save at least one life.

EATING FRUITS

It's long, but very informative.

We all think eating fruits means just buying fruits, cutting it, and just popping it into our mouths. It's more than that. It's important to know how and when to eat.

What is the correct way of eating fruits?

It means not eating fruits after your meals! fruits should be eaten on an empty stomach.

If you eat fruit like that, it will play a major role to detoxify your system, supplying you with a great deal of energy for weight loss and other life activities.

Fruit is the most important food. Let's say you eat two slices of bread and then a slice of fruit. The slice of fruit is ready to go straight through the stomach into the intestines, but it is prevented from doing so.

In the meantime, the whole meal rots, ferments, and turns to acid. The minute the fruit comes into contact with the food in the stomach and digestive juices, the entire mass of food begins to spoil.

So please eat your fruits on an empty stomach or before your meals! You have heard people complaining—every time I eat watermelon I burp, when I eat durian my stomach bloats up, when I eat a banana I feel like running to the toilet etc., actually all this will not arise if you eat the fruit on an empty stomach. The fruit mixes with the putrefying other food and produces gas and hence you will bloat!

Graying hair, balding, nervous outburst, and dark circles under the eyes—all these will not happen if you take fruits on an empty stomach.

There is no such thing as some fruits, like orange and lemon are acidic, because all fruits become alkaline in our body, according to Dr. Herbert Shelton who did research on this matter. If you have mastered the correct way of eating fruits, you have the secret of beauty, longevity, health, energy, happiness, and normal weight.

When you need to drink fruit juice, drink only fresh fruit juice, *not* from the cans. Don't even drink juice that has been heated up. Don't eat cooked fruits because you don't get the nutrients at all.

You only get to taste. Cooking destroys all the vitamins.

But eating a whole fruit is better than drinking the juice. If you should drink the juice, drink it mouthful by mouthful slowly, because you must let it mix with your saliva before swallowing it. You can go on a three-day fruit fast to cleanse your body. Just eat fruits and drink fruit juice throughout the three days, and you will be surprised when your friends tell you how radiant you look!

Kiwi: Tiny but mighty. This is a good source of potassium, magnesium, vitamin E, and fiber. It's vitamin C content is twice that of an orange.

Apple: An apple a day keeps the doctor away. Although an apple has a low vitamin C content, it has antioxidants and flavonoids which enhances the activity of vitamin C thereby helping to lower the risks of colon cancer, heart attack and stroke.

Strawberry: Protective Fruit. Strawberries have the highest total antioxidant power among major fruits and protect the body from cancer-causing, blood vessel-clogging free radicals.

Orange: Sweetest medicine. Taking two to four oranges a day may help keep cold away, lower cholesterol, prevent and dissolve kidney stones as well as lessens the risk of colon cancer.

Watermelon: Coolest thirst quencher. Composed of 92 percent water, it is also packed with a giant dose of glutathione, which helps boost our immune system. They are also a key source of lycopene, the cancer fighting oxidant. Other nutrients found in watermelon are vitamin C and potassium.

Guava and papaya: Top awards for vitamin C. They are the clear winners for their high vitamin C content. Guava is also rich in fiber, which helps prevent constipation. Papaya is rich in carotene; this is good for your eyes.

FOOD AS MEDICINE

药 补 不 如 食 补

Use [mouse] or space bar, to advance slides.....

When  blinks

- ## HEADACHE? EAT FISH!
  Eat plenty of fish -- fish oil helps prevent headaches.
  头痛？吃鱼吧！
  吃多多的鱼 -- 鱼油可帮助你预防头痛。

- So does ginger, which reduces inflammation and pain.
  还有生姜，它可以降低炎症及疼痛的发生。

- ## TO PREVENT STROKE, DRINK TEA!
  Prevent buildup of fatty deposits on artery walls
  with regular doses of tea. (actually, tea
  suppresses my appetite and keeps the pounds
  from invading....Green tea is great for our immune
  system)!

  饮茶可以有效的预防中风！
  经常饮茶可以预防动脉血管壁中的脂肪堆积。（实际上茶可以抑制食欲，保
  持体重…… 绿茶还益于增强我们的免疫力）

- ## INSOMNIA (CAN'T SLEEP?) HONEY!
  Use honey as a tranquilizer and sedative.
  失眠（睡不着？）蜂蜜！
  蜂蜜有着镇静安神的功效。

- ## HAY FEVER? EAT YOGURT!
  Eat lots of yogurt before pollen season.
  Also - eat honey from your area (local region)
  daily.
  花粉症？酸奶！
  在花粉传播旺盛的季节前，多吃些酸奶，还有每天吃些蜂蜜。

- ## ASTHMA? EAT ONIONS!!!!
  Eating onions helps ease constriction of bronchial
  tubes. (when I was young, my mother would make
  onion packs to place on our chest, helped the
  respiratory ailments and actually made us breathe
  better).
  哮喘？吃洋葱！！
  洋葱对支气管的收缩有很大的帮助。(小时候，妈妈将洋葱放在胸口上，这种做
  法对呼吸道的病症很有效，事实上它让我们呼吸得更加畅快。)

- **UPSET STOMACH? BANANAS - GINGER!!!!!**
Bananas will settle an upset stomach.
Ginger will cure morning sickness and nausea.
在为胃痛烦恼? 香蕉-生姜!
香蕉可以缓解胃痛，而生姜则可治疗晨吐及反胃。

- **ARTHRITIS? EAT FISH, TOO!!**
Salmon, tuna, mackerel and sardines actually prevent
arthritis. (fish has omega oils, good for our immune system)
关节炎? 还是吃鱼!
三文鱼，金枪鱼，鲭鱼还有沙丁鱼均可预防关节炎。
(鱼类含有丰富的Omega鱼油，对我们的免疫系统有着极大的好处.)

- **BONE PROBLEMS? EAT PINEAPPLE!!!**
Bone fractures and osteoporosis can be prevented by
the manganese in pineapple.
骨骼问题? 凤梨!
骨折及骨质疏松均可靠凤梨中的锰元素得到预防。

- **BLADDER INFECTION? DRINK CRANBERRY
JUICE!!!!**
High-acid cranberry juice controls harmful bacteria.
膀胱炎? 多喝点酸莓汁吧!
含酸度高的酸莓汁可控制体内有害细菌的滋长。

- ## PREMENSTRUAL SYNDROME? EAT CORNFLAKES!!!!

  Women can ward off the effects of PMS with cornflakes, which help reduce depression, anxiety and fatigue.

  女性生理期综合症？脆玉米片！

  多吃些脆玉米片吧，女性朋友您就可以避免生理期所带来的不适，它可以有效的缓解情绪上的低落，焦虑及疲劳。

- ## MEMORY PROBLEMS? EAT OYSTERS!

  Oysters help improve your mental functioning by supplying much-needed zinc.

  记忆力差？蚝！

  蚝中有着我们人类所需的大量的锌，锌可改善我们大脑机能。

- ## COLDS? EAT GARLIC!

  Clear up that stuffy head with garlic. (remember, garlic lowers cholesterol, too.)

  感冒？吃点大蒜吧！

  让　　　来使头脑清醒！记住，大蒜还可以降低胆固醇。

• COUGHING? USE RED PEPPERS!!

A substance similar to that found in the cough syrups is found in hot red pepper. Use red (cayenne) pepper with caution - it can irritate your tummy.

咳嗽? 红辣椒!

它含有类似于咳嗽药水的物质。但要小心使用，因为它会刺激胃部引起不适。

• BREAST CANCER? EAT wheat, bran and cabbage

Helps to maintain estrogen at healthy levels.

乳癌? 小麦, 麸皮, 卷心菜

它们可以帮助人体维持健康水平的雌激素。

• LUNG CANCER? EAT DARK GREEN AND ORANGE AND VEGGIES !!!

A good antidote is beta carotene, a form of Vitamin A found in dark green and orange vegetables.

肺癌? 多吃深绿色和橙色的食品，做个素食者吧！

β胡萝卜素是非常好的解毒剂，其所形成的维他命 在深绿色及橙色蔬菜中也都含有。

- # DIARRHEA? EAT APPLES!

Grate an apple with its skin, let it turn brown and eat it to cure this condition. (Bananas are also good for this ailment)

病疾？苹果！

将带皮的苹果烤成褐色之后吃下去会治愈病疾（香蕉对这一症状也很有效）

- # ULCERS? EAT CABBAGE ALSO!!!
Cabbage contains chemicals that help heal both gastric and duodenal ulcers.

溃疡？还是卷心菜！

卷心菜所含的化学成分有助于治疗胃溃疡以及十二指肠溃疡。

- # CLOGGED ARTERIES? EAT AVOCADO!
Mono unsaturated fat in avocados lowers cholesterol.

动脉阻塞？鳄梨果！

鳄梨果中的单元不饱和脂肪会降低体内胆固醇含量。

- # HIGH BLOOD PRESSURE? EAT CELERY AND OLIVE OIL!!!
Olive oil has been shown to lower blood pressure. Celery contains a chemical that lowers pressure too.

高血压？多吃芹菜和食用橄榄油！

橄榄油能降低血压，芹菜中所含的化学元素也有这一功效。

- BLOOD SUGAR IMBALANCE? EAT BROCCOLI AND PEANUTS!!!
  血糖不稳定？椰菜和花生！

- The chromium in broccoli and peanuts helps regulate insulin and blood sugar.
  椰菜和花生中中含有的铬元素有效的控制胰岛素以及血糖的含量。

• Kiwi: Tiny but mighty. This is a good source of potassium, magnesium, Vitamin E & fiber. It's Vitamin C content is twice that of an orange.
猕猴桃：个头小但作用大。含有丰富的钾，镁，维他命E以及纤维素。它的维他命C含量是橙的两倍。

• Apple: An apple a day keeps the doctor away? Although an apple has a low Vitamin C content, it has antioxidants & falconoid which enhances the activity of Vitamin C thereby helping to lower the risks of colon cancer, heart attack & stroke.
苹果：每天一个苹果可以不生病？
尽管苹果的维他命C含量不高，但是其所含的抗氧化剂和类黄酮能提高维他命C的活性，进而有助于降低直肠癌，心脏病和中风的发生率。

156

Strawberry: Protective fruit. Strawberries have the highest total antioxidant power among major fruits & protects the body from cancer causing, blood vessels clogging free radicals. (Actually, any berry is good for you. They're high in anti-oxidants and they actually keep us young.........blueberries are the best and very versatile in the health field........they get rid of all the free-radicals that invade our bodies)

草莓：具有防护功能的水果。草莓的抗氧化能力是水果之最，能从根本上预防癌症以及血管的堵塞。（实际上，任何浆果对人体都是有益的。他们均有高含量的抗氧化剂，能使我们青春永驻。蓝莓是最好也是万能的健康保护伞，它能有效地去除那些对身体不利的物质。）

Orange: Sweetest medicine. Taking 2 - 4 oranges a day may help keep colds away, lower cholesterol, prevent & dissolve kidney stones as well as lessen the risk of colon cancer.

橙：最甜的药。每天吃两到四只橙有助于预防感冒，降低胆固醇，溶解肾结石，并能降低直肠癌的发病率。

Watermelon: Coolest Thirst Quencher. Composed of 92% water, it is also packed with a giant dose of glutathione which helps boost our immune system. They are also a key source of lycopene - the cancer fighting oxidant. Other nutrients found in watermelon are Vitamin C & Potassium. (watermelon also has natural substances [natural SPF sources] that keep our skin healthy, protecting our skin from those darn suv rays)

西瓜：清爽的止渴水果。

西瓜中92%是水份，其所含有的大量谷胱甘肽可增加我们的免疫力，同时也是抗癌氧化剂 - 番茄红素的重要来源。西瓜中还有丰富的维他命C和钾。（西瓜是天然的防晒源，其所含的物质有效的抵抗紫外线，保持皮肤健康）

Guava & Papaya: Top awards for Vitamin C. They are the clear winners for their high Vitamin C content. Guava is also rich in fiber which helps prevent constipation.

番石榴和木瓜：富含大量维他命C，是水果中的维C之王。番石榴还含有大量的纤维素，能防止便秘。

- **Papaya** is rich in carotene, this is good for your eyes. (also good for gas and indigestion)
  木瓜富含胡萝卜素，对 有益。（对治疗消化不良和胀气也有帮助）

- **Tomatoes** are very good as a preventative measure for men, keeps those prostrate problems from invading their bodies.
  多吃番茄对男性而言起到很好的预防作用，能使身体充满活力。

Malunggay Benefits

The leaves of malunggay, dubbed miracle tree, have been discovered as the most nutritious bio food on earth. However, the seeds of malunggay are still hardly known as a highly promising source of biofuel (biodiesel).

The miracle leaves of malunggay contain four times the calcium and twice the protein of milk, seven times the vitamin C of oranges, four times the vitamin A (beta-carotene) of carrots, thrice the potassium in bananas, three times the iron content in spinach, with a full complement of minerals and all the amino acids of meat.

Three spoonfuls of malunggay leaf powder contain 272 percent of a typical toddler's daily vitamin A requirement, along with 42 percent of the protein, 125 percent of the calcium, 71 percent of the iron and 22 percent of the vitamin C.

Studies in the Philippines and many other countries have shown that malunggay is nature's medicine cabinet, with all the parts of the tree, besides the leaves, having medicinal or therapeutic value.

The leaves and flowers of malunggay are ideal for breastfeeding mothers and for malnourished children and the elderly. Using the leaves can also help in the treatment of headaches, bleeding from a shallow cut or wound, insect bites, bacterial or fungal skin complaints, gastric ulcers, and diarrhea.

The pods are useful in the treatment for worm, liver, spleen problems, and joint pains.

Malunggay has ninety phytonutrient compounds and is an excellent source of natural alternative (versus synthetic) vitamins and minerals.

The powdered malunggay leaves are cheaper, safer, and better than powdered whole milk, can rebuild weak bones, enrich anemic blood, and enable a malnourished mother to nurse her starving baby.

Doctors are known to treat diabetes in West Africa, high blood pressure in India, and malnutrition in Senegal, with malunggay.

In the Philippines, it is also known to fight cancer, and scientists have recently reported that it can hike male potency, with more sperm production.

The seeds of malunggay, when mixed with coconut oil or with its own seed oil, can be used to treat arthritis, rheumatism, gout, cramps, sexually transmitted disease (STD), urinary problems, epilepsy, and boils. The seeds are also effective for water purification or making contaminated water fit for drinking.

Many countries, including the Philippines, are now investing huge sums of money for biofuel development, but their main concern is that biofuel plants should not compete with food production, or making less food available to the people, like using corn and sugarcane for bioethanol production.

In the case of malunggay, it is like hitting two birds with one stone. The leaves of malunggay are quick and easy to grow in abundance, giving the most nutritious phytonutrients, while the seeds produce oil of the same volume as the popular jatropha curcas, of 38 percent to 40 percent oil, and even better quality.

Both malunggay and jatropha are perennial plants (trees) and can grow on marginal land, with minimal soil fertility and moisture.

Both can also have an economic life span of thirty to fifty years.

Natural Healer

How Dr. Wu rid himself of cancer with a vegetarian diet?
Anjira Assavanonda
Published: 7/05/2009
Newspaper section: Mylife

At the age of thirty, Chinese doctor, Tom Wu was diagnosed with advanced stages of lung cancer, and was told he had only a few months to live.

However, Dr. Wu, who recently spoke with Mylife, has already reached seventy years, and to our surprise, he still looks like a young and healthy man in his fifties.

Not only has he survived, but the doctor has maintained a healthy life. The cancer is all gone, and he said he's never caught a cold or other illness for forty years. He has stopped going for blood tests.

"My body and feelings tell me I'm well, that I'm truly in good health," says Dr. Wu.

His secret lies in the power of natural healing. Dr. Wu always says that no wonder drug can cure diseases. But our own internal healing power, our immune system, can. And what can strengthen our immune system are simple foods from Mother Nature, and a healthy lifestyle. In his view, diseases such as cancer, diabetes, and heart disease can be overcome by changing the diet.

Dr. Wu says people get sick because they eat the wrong foods. Fried food, for example, causes blockage in the arteries, bad circulation, cholesterol, and heart disease.

"Instead of taking a cholesterol lowering drug, I would urge them to stop eating greasy food. My suggestion is to eat clean food, which is high in phytochemicals," he says.

Phytochemicals are natural cleansing agents that will help rid plaque from your arteries. They come from natural foods such as vegetables, fruits with their seeds, and common garden herbs. Phytochemicals will nourish the body's cells so they can fight against any foreign substances that invade your body.

Dr. Wu's outstanding contributions to the development of natural medicine earned him the "World Famous Doctor Award" from the UN in 2001, and the "Best Wellness Doctor of the World" award from India's World Wellness Open University in March.

The secrets of how he won the fight against lung cancer and maintains a healthy body are revealed in his first book, *Dr. Wu's Principle of Natural Cures*, which has recently been translated from its original Chinese version into a Thai edition, *Thammachart Chuay Chewit*, published by Nanmeebooks Publications. It was launched in Thailand in March.

Dr. Wu says what's written in the book is unique and easy to understand because the author is both the doctor and the patient himself. All the ideas and guidelines suggested in the book come from his own experience as well as what he has learned from his patients.

Dr. Wu turns to natural medicine.

Dr. Wu had first studied Western medicine in France, and then furthered his education in alternative therapy, earning a doctorate degree.

The turning point arrived when he was diagnosed with lung cancer at the age of thirty. Modern medicine gave him no hope; it was too late to remove the damaged parts of the lung. The cancer had already spread to other organs, and the doctor told him he had only a few months left.

In his despair, Dr. Wu picked up the Bible and prayed to God. Then the Bible fell to the floor, and he read the page it opened to carefully. The chapter talked about the days God created the Earth and everything needed for human beings. Then he created Adam and Eve, and told both of them that plants, vegetables, and seeded fruits growing on earth have been provided for them to eat.

"I thought about what I had eaten in the past—meat, fish, fried and grilled food, sweet cake, but God simply wanted us to eat vegetables and sour fruits. I was confused and doubted whether I would become weak if I ate too many vegetables and less meat," says Dr Wu.

Yet he decided to follow the Bible's guidance. He ate a lot of vegetables and fruits, drank clean water, and completely adjusted his lifestyle—his sleeping, breathing, and exercise habits.

Nine months later, he went for a checkup, and surprisingly no cancer cells were detected.

He advised people in his family and in the neighborhood about his discovery, and studied natural medicine until he received a doctorate degree in naturopathy and nutrition from the United States.

Dr. Wu has been a frequent speaker at worldwide forums, spreading his knowledge on natural cures and the use of organic food. He advises people to use the most simple foods in the most natural way in order to fight illnesses and maintain good health.

The human body has the power to heal itself. The immune system has a self-defense mechanism to block and destroy bacteria or viruses that invade our bodies, while the self-healing mechanism will get us back on the road to recovery. When you have a cold and take medicine, the medication may kill the virus but your immune system will not fully function, and its efficiency will decrease. As a result, your body will be more vulnerable to germs.

Dr. Wu's principle is to strengthen the immune system, and avoid medication as much as possible. In his book, he offers the following guidelines to good health:

1. Have at least three bowel movements a day. Other health experts may advise one bowel movement a day, but Dr. Wu says that's not enough. You need three to four bowel movements a day in order to excrete all the accumulated feces from your intestine. Your liver will not be overburdened, and it also helps reduce cholesterol in your body.

2. Drink at least three glasses of fruit or vegetable smoothies each day. This is a way to ingest enough phytochemicals to strengthen the body's cells and immune system. Use not only the flesh, but also the skin and seeds of fruits and vegetables to make smoothies, as they are rich in phytochemicals. Most of the fruit seeds have small amounts of cyanide, which kill bacteria and viruses without damaging the body. Actually, the recommended smoothie diet is six glasses a day, two in the morning, one before lunch, two more in the afternoon, and one more before dinner. However, if that's too much, you may start with three glasses a day. Use a high-powered blender (at least three horsepower) as it can release phytochemicals from the fiber. It's best to choose sour fruits like green or red apples, grapes, pineapples, kiwi, and lime.

3. Sunbathe thirty minutes daily. We often hear that the Sun's UV rays will damage our skin, and many people apply sun block before going out. But Dr. Wu says the opposite. He says the UV rays will help convert cholesterol underneath the skin into vitamin A which helps moisten the skin and prevent skin cancer, and also vitamin D that helps prevent colds, osteoporosis, and certain kinds of cancer. "Therefore, use the sun. Expose yourself to sunlight about half an hour a day, at noon or another appropriate time based on your local climate. The sun will make you healthier," says Dr. Wu.

4. Exercise thirty minutes a day. Don't exercise for more than thirty minutes. If you go beyond that, your body will be overworked. "If you do it more than half an hour, that will become labor, not exercise. Your heart and your body will be working too hard," he says.

5. Shower with hot, then cold water. Try an alternating cold and hot water shower: Three minutes of hot water followed by thirty seconds of cold water, then repeat twice more. This process will bring a rush of blood and energy to your body. It helps increase your immune system, blood circulation, and metabolism.

6. Drink a lot of water, in the correct way. How much water you need to drink each day depends on your specific situation. If your office is air-conditioned, drinking six glasses of water a day is enough. If your work involves lots of walking, you have to drink eight to ten glasses a day. If you work under the hot sun, then ten to twelve glasses of water are required. The way you drink is also important. The correct way is to sip it little by little, to give your body cells time to absorb the water. If you drink the whole glass down at once, your cells can't absorb it all, and the water will be excreted as urine.

7. Eat according to your blood type. Your blood type determines what you should eat. Eating the wrong foods will make you sick. People with blood type O have to eat a certain amount of meat. If they eat only vegetables for a long time, their body won't absorb all the substances they need to strengthen their immune system. The recommended diet for this group is 75 percent vegetables, 10 percent fruits, 10 percent meat, seafood, and goat's milk (avoid cow's milk), and 5 percent grains. People with blood type A however should avoid milk and meat, while increasing grains and fruits. People with blood type B should also avoid meat, while those with blood type AB should avoid chicken and beef.

8. Eat according to your biological clock. Every human being has a biological clock that tells us when to eat, sleep, and wake up. If you don't follow your biological clock, the organs will lose their balance. Toxins and wastes won't be excreted from your body, and soon you'll get sick. According to Dr. Wu, the biological clock is divided into three phases. From 4:00 a.m. to noon is the time for bowel movements, so in the morning you should eat foods with lots of fiber. Fruit and vegetable smoothies are recommended. From noon to 8:00 p.m., your body will absorb food, so lunch is the most important meal. A vegetable salad with grains is recommended. Fish or boiled eggs can be added to your lunch. Avoid meat at dinner, as the amino acids in the meat will disturb your sleep. Try to finish dinner by 6:00 p.m. From 8:00 p.m. to 4:00 a.m., the nutrients and energy from food will be distributed throughout your body organs. The golden time for your sleep is between 10:00 p.m. and 2:00 a.m., as your immune and self-healing system will function at its best.

Aspire to inspire before you expire!

OVARIAN CANCER

Signs of Ovarian Cancer (even in the absence of Ovaries)—an Eye-Opener on Ovarian Cancer

Years ago, Gilda Radner died of ovarian cancer. Her symptoms were inconclusive, and she was treated for everything under the sun until it was too late. This blood test finally identified her illness but, alas, too late. She wrote a book to heighten awareness. Gene Wilder is her widower.

Kathy's Story: this is the story of Kathy West

I have primary peritoneal cancer. This cancer has only recently been identified as its *own* type of cancer, but it is essentially ovarian cancer.

Both types of cancer are diagnosed in the same way, with the tumor marker CA-125 *blood test*, and they are treated in the same way—surgery to remove the primary tumor and then chemotherapy with Taxol and Carboplatin.

Having gone through this ordeal, I want to save others from the same fate. That is why I am sending this message to you and hope you will print it and give it or send it via e-mail to everybody you know.

One thing I have learned is that each of us must take *total* responsibility for our own health care. I thought I had done that because I always had an annual physical and Pap smear, did a monthly self-breast exam, went to the dentist at least twice a year, etc. I even insisted on a sigmoidoscopy and a bone density test last year. When I had a total hysterectomy in 1993, I thought that I did not have to worry about getting any of the female reproductive organ cancers.

Little did I know, I don't have ovaries (and they were *healthy* when they were removed), but I have what is essentially ovarian cancer. Strange, isn't it?

These are just *some* of the things our doctors never tell us: *one* out of every fifty-five women will get *ovarian or primary peritoneal cancer.*

The *classic* symptoms are an *abdomen* that rather *suddenly enlarges* and *constipation* and/or *diarrhea.*

I had these classic symptoms and went to the doctor. Because these symptoms seemed to be abdominal, I went to a gastroenterologist. He ran tests that were designed to determine whether there was a bacteria infection; these tests were negative, and I was diagnosed with irritable bowel syndrome. I guess I would have accepted this diagnosis had it not been for my enlarged abdomen. I swear to you, it looked like I was four to five months pregnant! I therefore insisted on more tests.

They took an X-ray of my abdomen; it was negative. I was again assured that I had *Irritable Bowel Syndrome and was encouraged to go on my scheduled month-long trip to Europe. I couldn't wear any of my slacks or shorts because I couldn't get them buttoned, and *I knew* something was radically wrong. *I insisted* on more tests, and they reluctantly scheduled me for a CT scan (just to shut me up, I think). This is what I mean by taking charge of our own health care.

The CT scan showed a lot of fluid in my abdomen (*not* normal). Needless to say, I had to cancel my trip and have *five pounds* of fluid drawn off at the hospital (not a pleasant experience, I assure you), but *nothing* compared to what was ahead of me.

Tests revealed cancer cells in the fluid. Finally, finally, finally, the doctor ran a CA-125 blood test, and I was properly diagnosed.

I had the classic symptoms for ovarian cancer, and yet this simple CA-125 blood test had never been run on me, not as part of my annual physical exam and not when I was symptomatic. This is an inexpensive and simple blood test!

Please, please tell all your female friends and relatives to insist on a CA-125 blood test every year as part of their annual physical exams.

Be forewarned that their doctors might try to talk them out of it, saying, 'It isn't necessary.' Believe me, had I known then what I know now, we would have caught my cancer much earlier (before it was a stage three cancer). Insist on the CA-125 *blood test; do not* take *no* for an answer!

The normal range for a CA-125 *blood test* is between zero and thirty-five. *Mine was* 754. (That's right, 754!). If the number is slightly above thirty-five, you can have another done in three or six months and keep a close eye on it, just as women do when they have fibroid tumors, or when men have a slightly elevated PSA test (Prostatic Specific Antigens) that helps diagnose prostate cancer.

Having the CA-125 test done annually can alert you early, and that's the goal in diagnosing any type of cancer—catching it early.

Do you know fifty-five women? If so, at least one of them will have this *very aggressive* cancer. Please, go to your doctor and insist on a CA-125 test and have one *every year* for the rest of your life.

And forward this message to every woman you know, and tell all of your female family members and friends. Though the median age for this cancer is fifty-six, (and, guess what, I'm exactly fifty-six), women as young as twenty-two have it. Age is no factor.

A note from the RN:

Well, after reading this, I made some calls. I found that the CA-125 test is an ovarian screening test equivalent to a man's PSA test prostate screen (which my husband's doctor automatically gives him in his physical each year, and insurance pays for it). I called the general practitioner's office about having the test done. The nurse had never heard of it. She told me that she doubted that insurance would pay for it. So I called Prudential Insurance Co, and got the same response. Never heard of it—it won't be covered.

I explained that it was the same as the PSA test they had paid for my husband for years. After conferring with whomever they confer with, she told me that the CA-125 would be covered.

It is $75 in a GP's office and $125 at the GYN's. This is a screening test that should be required just like a PAP smear (a PAP smear cannot detect problems with your ovaries). And you must insist that your insurance company pay for it.

Gene Wilder and Pierce Brosnan (his wife had it, too) are lobbying for women's health issues, saying that this test should be required in our physicals, just like the PAP and the mammogram.

REMOVING GALLSTONES NATURALLY

Dr. Lai Chiu-Nan

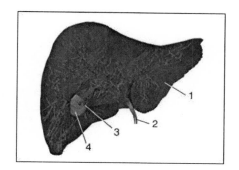

1. Liver
2. Common Bile Duct
3. Gallstones
4. Gallbladder

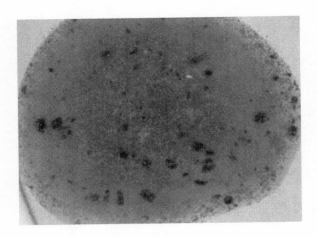

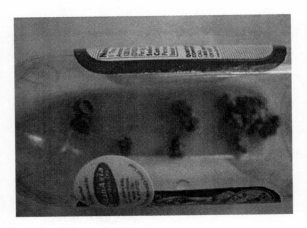

It has worked for many. If it works for you please pass on the good news. Chiu Nan is not charging for it, so we should make it free for everyone. Your reward is when someone, through your word of mouth, benefits from the regime. Gallstones may not be everyone's concern. But they should be because we all have them. Moreover, gallstones may lead to cancer. Cancer is never the first illness, Chiu Nan points out. Usually, there are a lot of other problems leading to cancer.

In my research in China, I came across some materials, which say that people with cancer usually have stones. We all have gallstones. It's a matter of big or small, many or few.

One of the symptoms of gallstones is a feeling of bloatedness after a heavy meal. You feel like you can't digest the food. If it gets more serious, you feel pain in the liver area. So if you think you have gallstones, Chiu Nan offers the following method to remove them naturally.

The treatment is also good for those with a weak liver, because the liver and gallbladder are closely linked.

Regimen:

1. For the first five days, take four glasses of apple juice every day. Or eat four or five apples, whichever you prefer. Apple juice softens the gallstones. During the five days, eat normally.

2. On the sixth day, take no dinner.

3. At 6:00 p.m., take a teaspoon of Epsom salt (magnesium sulphate) with a glass of warm water.

4. At 8:00 p.m., repeat the same. Magnesium sulphate opens the gallbladder ducts.

5. At 10:00 p.m., take half cup olive oil (or sesame oil) with half cup fresh lemon juice. Mix it well and drink it. The oil lubricates the stones to ease their passage.

PS. 1cup=250ml, 1 cup lemon juice=3 lemons (approx.)

The next morning, you will find green stones in your stools. "Usually they float," Chiu Nan notes. "You might want to count them. I have had people who pass forty, fifty, or up to hundred stones. Too many."

"Even if you don't have any symptoms of gallstones, you still might have some. It's always good to give your gall bladder a cleanup now and then."

RIPE BANANAS

Good Qualities of Ripe Bananas

Bananas with dark patches on yellow skin enhance the property of white cells and prevent cancer.

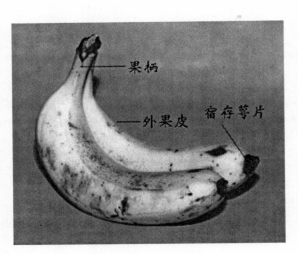

The fully ripe banana produces a substance called TNF, which has the ability to combat abnormal cells. So don't be surprised if fruit stands, and supermarkets will soon be out of stock for bananas.

As the banana ripens, it develops dark spots or patches on the skin. The more dark patches it has, the higher will be its immunity enhancement quality. Hence, the Japanese love bananas for a good reason.

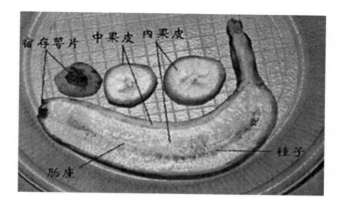

In an animal experiment carried out by a professor in Tokyo University comparing the various health benefits of different fruits, using banana, grape, apple, watermelon, pineapple, pear, and persimmon, it was found that banana gave the best results. It increased the number of white blood cells, enhanced the immunity of the body, and produced anticancer substance TNF.

The recommendation is to eat one to two bananas a day to increase your body immunity to diseases like cold, flu, and others.

According to the Japanese professor, yellow skin bananas with dark spots on it are eight times more effective in enhancing the property of white blood cells than the green skin version.

So my friends, let's go bananas!

Secrets to a Sound Night's Sleep

Restful sleep is more than a luxury, it's critical to your health. Sleep is the *only* chance your body gets to repair and rejuvenate, and get you mentally prepared for a new day. So, as you can imagine, a lack of sleep can affect your productivity, creativity, and alertness—not to mention your mood!

If you're finding it tougher to fall asleep and stay asleep, you're not alone. As you get older, and especially during menopause, sound sleep can become more elusive. This is particularly true if you're suffering from hot flashes and night sweats. Plus, stress and anxiety play a big role in how well you sleep.

The common, conventional approach to promoting better sleep is prescription medication. However, I don't believe these drugs are an effective long-term solution, and can even be dangerously addictive. Instead, I suggest a more natural approach, including my recommendations below.

Bedtime Rules

Your lifestyle plays a huge role in how well you sleep. Do you have regular diet, exercise, and sleep habits? If not, it may be time to make some changes. In addition, it helps to create as comfortable and peaceful an environment in your bedroom as possible. These tips can help get you started.

Maintain a regular sleep schedule—even on weekends. Your sleep/wake cycle is regulated by an internal clock in your brain that functions best when its sleep time and wake time is balanced. By waking up and going to bed at the same time every day, you strengthen this clock.

Establish a bedtime routine. Do something relaxing every night before bed, such as taking a hot bath, massaging your feet, or listening to classical music.

Set the right environment. Keep your bedroom quiet, dark, and free of possible interruptions. Devices are available to create *white noise,* such as the gentle sound of rain and ocean waves, to help keep distractions at a minimum and lull you to sleep.

Make sure you're sleeping on a supportive bed. Use a mattress topper that adds extra cushion and support for your entire body.

Don't eat within three hours of bedtime. Eating heavy meals late in the day can cause stomach discomfort, gas, or occasional bloating. I always try to eat before 7:00 p.m. unless I'm going to a party or out to dinner. Also, be sure to avoid caffeine (which can keep you up) and alcohol (which can cause you to have restless sleep).

Exercise regularly. Late afternoon workouts—at least thirty minutes a day—are ideal for encouraging sounder, deeper, more restful sleep. Be sure to finish your workout at least three hours before bed, as it takes several hours for your body to cool down sufficiently.

Take Sleep Promoting Supplements. There are several nutrients that are all-natural, nonaddictive, and completely safe for promoting a sound night's sleep. They include:

L-theanine: This fat-soluble amino acid, found almost exclusively in tea plants, has a calming effect that helps to relax your mind and induce sleep. You want to take 200 mg before bed.

Melatonin: This hormone is naturally released by the pituitary gland at night and dictates your sleep patterns. Around age forty, our melatonin levels naturally decline. By supplementing with melatonin, you can get your sleep patterns back in balance—so you fall asleep faster, and stay asleep. Research shows that 3 mg of melatonin is most effective.

5-HTP: Your body uses this amino acid to create serotonin, the feel-good hormone, which helps to erase tension and promote good sleep. I recommend taking 30 mg of 5-HTP.

Acupressure is based on the traditional Chinese belief that the body contains a life energy called chi—that runs through the body in channels called meridians. Restoring normal chi helps heal your body and promote good health. Acupressure involves applying gentle finger pressure to specific points on your skin to help restore chi.

The two points traditionally used to help promote sleep are the Spirit Gate and Inner Gate. The Spirit Gate is located on the inside of your wrist crease, in line with your little finger. The Inner Gate is located in the middle of the inner side of your forearm, two and one-half finger widths from your wrist. To promote restful sleep, apply pressure to each of these points, one at a time, for about thirty seconds. Remember to apply pressure to these spots on both sides of your body.

Lack of restful sleep can be a sign of an underlying condition. If the advice I've provided does not help you achieve a good night's sleep, I recommend that you contact your doctor.

Here's to your good health—and a restful night's sleep!

Susan M Lark M.D.

Susan M. Lark, MD

SODA AND YOUR KIDNEY

Article from Bottom Line's Daily Health News

There's just nothing to be gained from drinking soda. Think about it—people don't hesitate to drink what is basically a bubbly brew of water, sugar (mainly high fructose corn syrup or HFCS), food coloring and assorted chemicals, packed with calories and lacking in nutritional value.

Carbonated soft drinks are the single largest source of calories in the American diet, according to the Center for Science in the Public Interest, providing about 7 percent of our total calorie intake. In addition to staining, eroding, and decaying our teeth, soft drinks are associated with an increased risk of obesity, a risk factor for type 2 diabetes and possibly osteoporosis. Now there is a new health problem to add to that list—kidney damage.

More soda = more sugar = more risk

In a study of 9,358 adults (mean age forty-five), women who reported drinking two or more sugary sodas within the last twenty-four hours were nearly twice as likely to have albuminuria—excess levels of a protein in the urine that is a possible sign of kidney damage. More research is needed to determine if the association with kidney damage is due to sugar in general . . . HFCS in particular . . . or some shared lifestyle characteristics of soda drinkers.

Here's what we know so far . . .

- The widespread use of high fructose corn syrup, popular with manufacturers because it is cheap, sweet, and extends shelf life, has been prevalent over the same time period there's been a significant rise in diabetic end-stage renal or kidney disease. The body processes HFCS differently than regular table sugar, and in so doing may cause harm to the kidneys.

- Mercury has been detected in many products containing HFCS. (For more on this newly identified hazard, see Daily Health News, *April 27, 2009*.) Mercury is involved in the manufacturing process for most commercial HFCS—and mercury is a risk for kidney disease.

- Other ingredients in soda, such as phosphorus in colas, may contribute to kidney stones, which are a risk factor for chronic kidney disease.

- Men did not have this problem (more research is needed to learn why). Neither did people of either gender that drank diet soda, which is one reason why investigators believe HFCS may be responsible. Results of this research were published in the October 2008, issue of PLoS ONE.

Drink Water

To protect your kidneys, your best bet is to simply drink water instead of soda, advises lead researcher David Shoham, PhD, MSPH, of the Loyola University Health System in Illinois. Soda just isn't worth it.

Source(s):

David Shoham, PhD, MSPH, assistant professor, department of preventive medicine and epidemiology, Loyola University Health System, Maywood, Illinois.

Be well,

Carole Jackson
Bottom Line's *Daily Health News*

Stress Management Technique

Stress Management is more than anger management and relaxation. It is self-management. There are many different ways to manage stress. I have compiled the various stress management techniques that are simple and most effective to follow and practice. Please feel free to use as many as you can, keeping an open mind, so you can have a collection of techniques that are the most effective for you.

Feel Good about Yourself

If you want to bring down your level of stress in a matter of minutes, these techniques will help you. Use them as needed to feel better quickly; practice them regularly over time and gain even greater benefits.

- Deep breathing from the abdomen
- Meditation
- Having a dose of laughter
- Progressive muscular relaxation
- Listening to light music
- Practicing yoga
- Aerobic exercises
- Creative visualization

Take Care of Your Body

When we're stressed, we don't always take care of our bodies, which can lead to even more stress. Here are some important ways to take care of yourself and keep stress levels lower.

- Eat healthy low fats, high protein meals
- Have six to eight hours of regular sleep
- Exercise regularly
- Develop a hobby

Develop the Right Attitude

Attitude plays a great role in managing stress. Much of your experience of stress has a lot to do with your attitude and the way you perceive your life's events. Here are some resources to help you maintain a stress-relieving attitude.

- Let go of your ego
- Have an optimistic approach to life
- Do not react under pressure
- Stop worrying about things not in your control
- Accept that everything cannot be perfect
- Find an opportunity in every problem
- Say good things to your self-affirmations
- Have a healthy sense of humor

Develop the Right Environment

Having ambience and pleasant environment makes stress management very easy. Your physical and emotional surroundings can impact your stress levels in subtle but significant ways. Here are several ways you can change your atmosphere and lessen your stress.

- Clutter free home, office, and working desk
- Green and clean surrounding
- Light instrumental music
- Motivational posters
- Words of wisdom

Short Tips for Busy People

Busy people add a lot of stress to their already stressed life. People who may have more stressors in their lives is because they have more activity in their lives, and less time to devote to stress management. If you're a busy person, these resources can help you to manage stress efficiently in a short amount of time, and eliminate some of what's causing you stress in the first place.

- Time management tips
- Communication skills
- Listening skills
- Managing priorities
- Enhancing team work
- Enhancing people skills

THE BENEFITS OF SEX

The BENEFITS of SEX

Reading this is entertaining !!!

Be sure to read the final comment.

*Did you know that we can determine if a
person is sexually active or not by looking
at her skin?*

*1. Sex is a beauty treatment. Scientific tests have shown that a
woman who has sexual relations produces big amounts of
estrogen which makes hair shiny and soft.*

2. *To make love in soft and relaxed way reduces the possibilities of suffering from dermatitis and acne. The sweat produced cleans pores and makes the skin shine.*

3. *To make love allows to burn all the calories accumulate is this romantic love scene.*

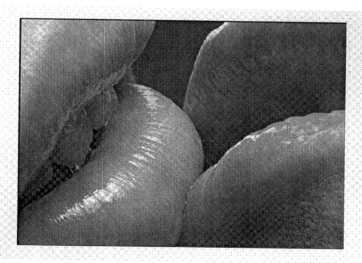

4. Sex is one of the safest sports. It strengthens and tonifies all body muscles. It is more enjoyable than doing 20 lapses in the pool. And you don't need special shoes!

5. Sex is an instantaneous cure against depression. It frees endorphines in the blood flow, creating a state of euphoria and leaves us with a feeling of well-being.

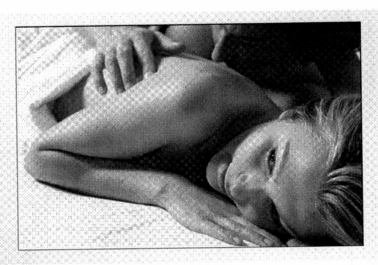

6. The more we make love, the more we have the capacity to do more. A Body sexually active releases a higher amount of pheromone. This subtle aroma excites the opposite sex!

7. Sex is the safest tranquiliser in the world. IT IS 10 TIMES MORE EFFICIENT THAN VALIUM.

8. *To kiss everyday allows to avoid the dentist. Kisses aid saliva in cleaning teeths and lower the quantity of acids causing enamel weakening.*

9. *Sex relieves headaches. Each time we make love, it releases the tension in brain veins.*

10. To make love a lot can heal a nasal congestion. Sex is a natural antihistaminic. It helps fight asthma and spring allergies.

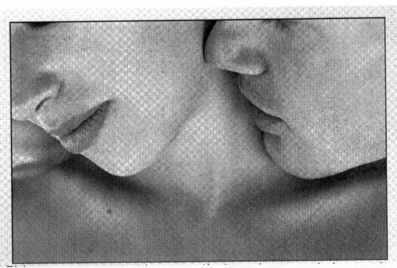

This message was sent to you so that you have good chances in sexual relations. It went around the world 9 times. It now arrived to you so that you can in turn enjoy "Benefits from Sex".

She will visit you 4 days after you have received this message, but only if you circulate it. If you do not, then you will never have good sexual relations again for the rest of your life. You will be celibate and your genital organs will rotten and fall off.

He Sends copies to whoever needs sex (who does not need any?). Do not send money, since the destiny of his genital organs does not have a price.

Do not keep this message. It must dissappear from your mailbox in 96 hours. Send 10 copies and see what happens in 4 days. This message must go around the world, so you must send it!!!
This is the truth, even if you are not superstitious. Good sex, but remember: 10 copies of this message must be sent in 96 hours or never again in your life will you have good sexual relations!!!

The Food Additive MSG

The food additive MSG (monosodium glutamate) is a low poison. MSG hides behind twenty-five or more names, such as Natural Flavoring. MSG is even in your favorite coffee from Tim Horton's and Starbucks coffee shops!

I wondered if there could be an actual chemical using the massive obesity epidemic, and so did a friend of mine, John Erb. He was a research assistant at the University of Waterloo in Ontario, Canada, and spent years working for the government. He made an amazing discovery while going through scientific journals for a book he was writing called *The Slow Poisoning of America*.

In hundreds of studies around the world, scientists were creating obese mice and rats to use in diet or diabetes test studies. No strain of rat or mice is naturally obese, so scientists have to create them.

They make these creatures morbidly obese by injecting them with MSG when they are first born.

The MSG triples the amount of insulin the pancreas creates, causing rats (and perhaps humans) to become obese. They even have a name for the fat rodents they create: "MSG-Treated Rats."

When I heard this, I was shocked. I went into my kitchen and checked the cupboards and the refrigerator. MSG was in everything—the Campbell's soups, the Hostess Doritos, the Lays flavored potato chips, Top Ramen, Betty Crocker Hamburger Helper, Heinz canned gravy, Swanson frozen prepared meals, and Kraft salad dressings, especially the *healthy low-fat* ones and most it's in the food of most Chinese Restaurants. (Doesn't sound like very healthy food choices in her cupboards and refrigerator to begin with!)

The items that didn't have MSG marked on the product label had something called "Hydrolyzed Vegetable Protein," which is just another name for monosodium glutamate.

It was shocking to see just how many of the foods we feed our children everyday are filled with this stuff. MSG is hidden under many different names in order to fool those who read the ingredient list, so that they don't catch on. (Other names for MSG are Accent, Ajinomoto, Natural Meat Tenderizer, etc.) But it didn't stop there.

When our family went out to eat, we started asking at the restaurants what menu items contained MSG. Many employees, even the managers, swore they didn't use MSG. But when we ask for the ingredient list, which they grudgingly provided, sure enough, MSG and Hydrolyzed Vegetable Protein were everywhere.

Burger King, McDonald's, Wendy's, Taco Bell, every restaurant—even the sit-down eateries like TGIF, Chili's, Applebee's, and Denny's, use MSG in abundance. Kentucky Fried Chicken seemed to be the *worst* offender: MSG was in every chicken dish, salad dressing, and gravy. No wonder I loved to eat that coating on the skin—their secret spice was MSG!

So why is MSG in so many of the foods we eat? Is it a preservative, or a vitamin?

Not according to my friend John Erb. In his book *The Slow Poisoning of America,* he said that MSG is added to food for the addictive effect it has on the human body.

Even the propaganda Web site sponsored by the food manufacturers lobby group supporting MSG explains that the reason they add it to food is to make people eat more.

A study of the elderly showed that older people eat more of the foods that it is added to. The Glutamate Association lobbying group says eating more is a benefit to the elderly, but what does it do to the rest of us?

"Betcha can't eat [just] one," takes on a whole new meaning where MSG is concerned! And we wonder why the nation is overweight!

MSG manufacturers themselves admit that it addicts people to their products. It makes people choose their product over others, and makes people eat more of it than they would if MSG wasn't added.

Not only is MSG scientifically proven to cause obesity, it is an addictive substance. Since its introduction into the American food supply fifty years ago, MSG has been added in larger and larger doses to the prepackaged meals, soups, snacks, and fast foods, we are tempted to eat everyday.

The FDA has set no limits on how much of it can be added to food. They claim it's safe to eat in any amount. But how can they claim it's safe when there are hundreds of scientific studies with titles like these:

> "The monosodium glutamate (MSG) obese rat as a model for the study of exercise in obesity."
> > Gobatto CA, Mello MA, Souza CT, Ribeiro IA. Res Commun Mol Pathol Pharmacol. 2002.

> "Adrenalectomy abolishes the food-induced hypothalamic serotonin release in both normal and monosodium glutamate-obese rats."
> > Guimaraes RB, Telles MM, Coelho VB, Mori C, Nascimento CM, Ribeiro. Brain Res Bull. 2002 Aug.

> "Obesity induced by neonatal monosodium glutamate treatment in spontaneously hypertensive rats: An animal model of multiple risk factors."
> > Iwase M, Yamamoto M, Iino K, Ichikawa K, Shinohara N, Yoshinari Fujishima. Hypertens Res. 1998 Mar.

> "Hypothalamic lesion induced by injection of monosodium glutamate in suckling period and subsequent development of obesity."
> > Tanaka K, Shimada M, Nakao K Kusunoki. Exp Neurol. 1978 Oct.

No, the date of that last study was not a typo; it was published in 1978. Both the medical research community and food manufacturers have known about the side effects of MSG for decades.

Many more of the studies mentioned in John Erb's book link MSG to diabetes, migraines, and headaches, autism, ADHD, and even Alzheimer's.

So what can we do to stop the food manufactures from dumping this fattening and addictive MSG into our food supply and causing the obesity epidemic we now see?

Several months ago, John Erb took his book and his concerns to one of the highest government health officials in Canada. While he was sitting in the government office, the official told him, "Sure, I know how bad MSG is. I wouldn't touch the stuff." But this top-level government official refuses to tell the public what he knows.

The big media doesn't want to tell the public either, fearing issues with their advertisers. It seems that the fallout on the fast food industry may hurt their profit margin. The food producers and restaurants have been addicting us to their products for years, and now we are paying the price for it. Our children should not be cursed with obesity caused by an addictive food additive.

But what can I do about it? I'm just one voice! What can I do to stop the poisoning of our children, while our governments are insuring financial protection for the industry that is poisoning us?

This message is going out to everyone I know in an attempt to tell you the truth that the corporate-owned politicians and media won't tell you.

The best way you can help to save yourself and your children from this drug-induced epidemic is to forward this article to everyone. With any luck, it will circle the globe before politicians can pass the legislation, protecting those who are poisoning us.

The food industry learned a lot from the tobacco industry. Imagine if big tobacco had a bill like this in place before someone was able to blow the whistle on nicotine?

If you are one of the few who can still believe that MSG is good for us, and you don't believe what John Erb has to say, see for yourself. Go to the national Library of Medicine at www.pubmed.com. Type in the words "MSG Obese" and read a few of the 115 medical studies that appear.

We the public do not want to be rats in one giant experiment and we do not approve of food that makes us into a nation of obese, lethargic, addicted sheep, feeding the food industry's bottom line while waiting for the heart transplant, the diabetic-induced amputation, blindness, or other obesity-induced, life-threatening disorders.

With your help, we can put an end to this poison. Do your part in sending this message out by word of mouth, e-mail, or by distribution of this printout to your friends all over the world and stop this "slow poisoning of mankind" by the packaged food industry.

Blowing the whistle on MSG is our responsibility, so get the word out.

Unhealthy Foods and Habits

Cancer Causing Foods

Hot dogs

Because they are high in nitrates, the Cancer Prevention Coalition advises that children eat no more than twelve hot dogs a month. If you can't live without hot dogs, buy those made without sodium nitrate.

Processed Meats and Bacon

Also high in the same sodium nitrates found in hot dogs, bacon, and other processed meats raise the risk of heart disease. The saturated fat in bacon also contributes to cancer.

Doughnuts

Doughnuts are cancer-causing double trouble. First, they are made with white flour, sugar, and hydrogenated oils, then fried at high temperatures. Doughnuts, says Adams, may be the worst food you can possibly eat to raise your risk of cancer.

French Fries and Chips

Like doughnuts, french fries are made with hydrogenated oils and then fried at high temperatures. They also contain cancer-causing acryl amides, which occur during the frying process. They should be called cancer fries, not french fries, said Adams.

Brain Damaging Habits

1. No Breakfast

People who do not take breakfast are going to have a lower blood sugar level. This leads to an insufficient supply of nutrients to the brain causing brain degeneration.

2. Overeating

Overeating causes hardening of the brain arteries, leading to a decrease in mental power.

3. Smoking

It causes multiple brain shrinkage and may lead to Alzheimer's disease.

4. High Sugar Consumption

Too much sugar will interrupt the absorption of proteins and nutrients causing malnutrition and may interfere with brain development.

5. Air Pollution

The brain is the largest oxygen consumer in our body. Inhaling polluted air decreases the supply of oxygen to the brain, bringing about a decrease in brain efficiency.

6. Sleep Deprivation

Sleep allows our brain to rest. Long-term deprivation from sleep will accelerate the death of brain cells.

7. Head Covered While Sleeping

Sleeping with the head covered increases the concentration of carbon dioxide and decrease concentration of oxygen that may lead to brain damaging effects.

8. Working Your Brain During Illness

Working hard or studying with sickness may lead to a decrease in effectiveness of the brain as well as damage the brain.

9.   Talking Rarely

Intellectual conversations will promote the efficiency of the brain.

10. Lacking in Stimulating Thoughts

Thinking is the best way to train our brain, lacking in brain stimulation thoughts may cause brain shrinkage.

Liver Damaging Habits

1.   Sleeping too late and waking up too late.

2.   Not urinating in the morning.

3.   Eating too much.

4.   Skipping breakfast.

5.   Taking too much medication.

6.   Consuming too much preservatives, additives, food coloring, and artificial sweetener.

7.   Consuming unhealthy cooking oil or too much cooking oil.

8.   Consuming raw or overly done foods.

9.   Consuming leftover fried veggies.

WATER VERSUS COKE

Water

1. 75 percent of Americans are chronically dehydrated (likely applies to half the world population.)

2. In 37 percent of Americans, the thirst mechanism is so weak that it is mistaken for hunger.

3. Even *mild* dehydration will slow down one's metabolism as 3 percent.

4. One glass of water shut down midnight hunger pangs for almost 100 percent of the dieters studied in a University of Washington study.

5. Lack of water, the number one trigger of daytime fatigue.

6. Preliminary research indicates that eight to ten glasses of water a day could significantly ease back and joint pain for up to 80 percent of sufferers.

7. A mere 2 percent drop in body water can trigger fuzzy short-term memory, trouble with basic math, and difficulty focusing on the computer screen or on a printed page.

8. Drinking 5 glasses of water daily *decreases* the risk of colon cancer by 45 percent, plus it can *slash the risk of breast cancer* by 79 percent., and one is 50 percent *less likely to develop bladder cancer.* Are you drinking the amount of water you should drink every day?

Coke

1. In many states, the highway patrol carries two gallons of Coke in the trunk to remove blood from the highway after a car accident.

2. You can put a T-bone steak in a bowl of Coke, and it will be gone in two days.

3. To clean a toilet: Pour a can of Coca-Cola into the toilet bowl and let the *real thing* sit for one hour, then flush clean. The citric acid in Coke removes stains from vitreous china.

4. To remove rust spots from chrome car bumpers: Rub the bumper with a rumpled-up piece of Reynolds Wrap aluminum foil dipped in Coca-Cola.

5. To clean corrosion from car battery terminals: Pour a can of Coca-Cola over the terminals to bubble away the corrosion.

6. To loosen a rusted bolt: Apply a cloth soaked in Coca-Cola to the rusted bolt for several minutes.

7. To bake a moist ham: Empty a can of Coca-Cola into the baking pan, wrap the ham in aluminum foil, and bake. Thirty minutes before ham is finished, remove the foil, allowing the drippings to mix with the Coke for a sumptuous brown gravy.

8. To remove grease from clothes: Empty a can of Coke into the load of greasy clothes, add detergent, and run through a regular cycle. The Coca-Cola will help loosen grease stains. It will also clean road haze from your windshield.

For Your Information:

1. The active ingredient in Coke is phosphoric acid. It will dissolve a nail in about four days. Phosphoric acid also leaches calcium from bones and is a major contributor to the rising increase of osteoporosis.

2. To carry Coca-Cola syrup (concentrate), the commercial trucks must use a hazardous material place cards reserved for highly corrosive materials.

3. The distributors of Coke have been using it to clean engines of the trucks for about twenty years!

Now the question is, would you like a glass of water or a glass of Coke?

ABOUT HUMOR

BLONDE MEETS BLONDE

A blonde woman was speeding down the road in her little yellow bug and was pulled over by a woman police officer who was also a blonde.

The blonde cop asked to see the blonde driver's license. She dug through her purse and was getting progressively more agitated.

"What does it look like?" She finally asked.

The policewoman replied, "It is square, and it has your picture on it."

The driver finally found a square mirror in her purse, looked at it, and handed it to the policewoman.

"Here it is," she said.

The blonde officer looked at the mirror, then handed it back saying, "Okay, you can go. I didn't realize you were a cop."

DEALING WITH NEGATIVITY

Here is something to think about when negative people are doing their best to rain on your parade. Remember this story the next time someone who knows nothing (and cares less) tries to make your life miserable . . .

A woman was at her hairdresser's getting her hair styled for a trip to Rome with her husband. She mentioned the trip to the hairdresser, who responded, "Rome? Why would anyone want to go there? It's crowded and dirty. You're crazy to go to Rome. So, how are you getting there?"

"We're taking Continental," was the reply. "We got a great rate!"

"Continental?" exclaimed the hairdresser. "That's a terrible airline. Their planes are old, their flight attendants are ugly, and they're always late. So, where are you staying in Rome?"

"We'll be at this exclusive little place over on Rome's Tiber River called Teste."

"Don't go any further. I know that place. Everybody thinks it's gonna be something special and exclusive, but it's really a dump."

"We're going to go to see the Vatican and maybe get to see the Pope."

"That's rich," laughed the hairdresser. "You and a million other people trying to see him. He'll look the size of an ant. Boy, good luck on this lousy trip of yours. You're going to need it."

A month later, the woman again came in for a hairdo. The hairdresser asked about her trip to Rome.

"It was wonderful," explained the woman, "not only were we on time in one of Continental's brand new planes, but it was overbooked, and they bumped us up to first class. The food and wine were wonderful, and I had a handsome twenty-eight-year-old steward who waited on me hand and foot.

"And the hotel was great! They'd just finished a $5 million remodeling job, and now it's a jewel, the finest hotel in the city. They, too, were overbooked, so they apologized and gave us their owner's suite at no extra charge!"

"Well," muttered the hairdresser, "that's all well and good, but I know you didn't get to see the Pope."

"Actually, we were quite lucky, because as we toured the Vatican, a Swiss guard tapped me on the shoulder, and explained that the Pope likes to meet some of the visitors, and if I'd be so kind as to step into his private room and wait, the Pope would personally greet me.

"Sure enough, five minutes later, the Pope walked through the door and shook my hand! I knelt down and he spoke a few words to me."

"Oh, really! What'd he say?"

He said, "Who fucked up your hair?"

Dr. Epstein

Dr. Epstein was a renowned physician who earned his undergraduate, graduate, and medical degrees in his hometown and then left for Manhattan, where he quickly rose to the top.

Soon he was invited to deliver a significant paper, at a conference, coincidentally held in his hometown. He walked on stage and placed his papers on the lectern, but they slid off onto the floor. As he bent over to retrieve them, at precisely the wrong instant, he inadvertently passed gas. The microphone amplified his mistake resoundingly through the room, and it reverberated down the hall! He was quite embarrassed but somehow regained his composure just enough to deliver his paper. He ignored the resounding applause and raced out the stage door, never to be seen in his hometown again.

Decades later, when his elderly mother was ill, he returned to visit her. He reserved a hotel room under the name of Levy and arrived under cover of darkness. The desk clerk asked him, "Is this your first visit to our city, Mr. Levy?" Dr. Epstein replied, "Well, young man, no, it isn't. I grew up here and received my education here, but then I moved away."

"Why haven't you visited?" asked the desk clerk.

"Actually, I did visit once, many years ago, but an embarrassing thing happened and since then I've been too ashamed to return."

The clerk consoled him. "Sir, while I don't have your life experience, one thing I have learned is that often what seems embarrassing to me isn't even remembered by others. I bet that's true of your incident too."

Dr. Epstein replied, "Son, I doubt that's the case with my incident." "Was it a long time ago?" asked the clerk. "Yes, many years," replied Dr. Epstein.

The clerk asked, "Was it before or after the Epstein fart?"

Ducks in Heaven

Three women die together in an accident and go to heaven.

When they get there, St. Peter says, "we only have one rule here in heaven: don't step on the ducks!"

So they enter heaven, and sure enough, there are ducks all over the place.

It is almost impossible not to step on a duck, and although they try their best to avoid them, the first woman accidentally steps on one.

Along comes St. Peter with the ugliest man she ever saw.

St. Peter chains them together and says, "Your punishment for stepping on a duck is to spend eternity chained to this ugly man!"

The next day, the second woman steps accidentally on a duck and along comes St. Peter, who doesn't miss a thing.

With him is another extremely ugly man. He chains them together with the same admonishment as for the first woman.

The third woman has observed all this and, not wanting to be chained for all eternity to an ugly man, is very, very careful where she steps.

She manages to go months without stepping on any ducks, but one day St. Peter comes up to her with the most handsome man she has ever laid eyes on . . . very tall, long eyelashes, muscular.

St. Peter chains them together without saying a word.

The happy woman says, "I wonder what I did to deserve being chained to you for all of eternity?"

The guy says, "I don't know about you, but I stepped on a duck."

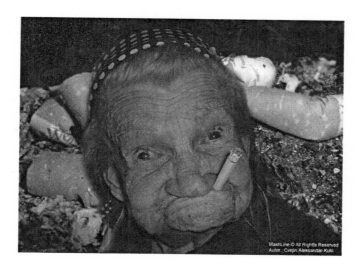

How to Deal with the Police if You're Old

George Phillips, age eighty-two, of Meridian, Mississippi was going up to bed, when his wife told him that he'd left the light on in the garden shed, which she could see from the bedroom window. George opened the back door to go turn off the light, but saw that there were people in the shed stealing things.

He phoned the police, who asked, "Is there someone in your house?" He said, "No." Then they said, "All patrols are busy. You should lock your doors, and an officer will be along when one is available." George said, "Okay." He hung up the phone and counted to thirty.

Then he phoned the police again. "Hello, I just called you a few seconds ago because there were people stealing things from my shed. Well, you don't have to worry about them now because I just shot them." He then hung up.

Within five minutes, six police cars, a SWAT team, a helicopter, two fire trucks, a paramedic, and an ambulance showed up at the Phillips' residence, and caught the burglars red-handed. One of the policemen said to George, "I thought you said that you shot them!"

George said, "I thought you said there was nobody available!" (true story)

IT'S MILKING TIME AGAIN

THE MODEL OF A BAILOUT PLAN

Once upon a time, a man appeared in a village and announced to the villagers that he would buy monkeys for $10 each. The villagers, knowing there were many monkeys, went to the forest, and started catching them. The man bought thousands at $10 and, as supply started to diminish, the villagers stopped their effort.

He then announced that he would buy monkeys at $20 each. This renewed the villagers', efforts, and they started catching monkeys again.

Soon the supply diminished and people started going back to their farms. The offer increased to $25 each, and the supply of monkeys became so scarce that it was an effort to even find a monkey, let alone catch it!

The man now announced that he would buy monkeys at $50 each! However, since he had to go to the city on some business, his assistant would buy on his behalf.

The assistant told the villagers, "Look at all these monkeys in the big cage that my boss has already collected. I will sell them to you at $35 and when my boss returns, you can sell them to him for $50."

The villagers rounded up all their savings and bought all the monkeys for seven hundred billion dollars.

They never saw the man or his assistant again, only lots and lots of monkeys!

THE OTHER TOILET

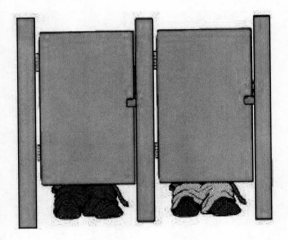

This could happen to you.

I was barely sitting down when I heard a voice from the other toilet saying, "Hi, how are you?"

I'm not the type to start a conversation in the restroom, but I don't know what got into me, so I answered, somewhat embarrassed, "Doin' just fine!"

And the other person says, "So what are you up to?"

What kind of question is that? At that point, I was thinking this is too bizarre so I say, "Uhhh, I'm like you, just traveling!"

At this point, I am just trying to get out as fast as I can when I hear another question, "Can I come over?"

Okay, this question is just too weird for me, but I figured I could just be polite and end the conversation. I tell him "No. I'm a little busy right now!"

Then I hear the person say nervously, "Listen, I'll have to call you back. There's an idiot in the other toilet who keeps answering all my questions."

Mobile phones, don't you just love them!

Vatican Humor

After getting all of Pope Benedict's luggage loaded into the limo, (and he doesn't travel light), the driver notices the Pope is still standing on the curb.

"Excuse me, Your Holiness," says the driver, "Would you please take your seat so we can leave?"

"Well, to tell you the truth," says the Pope, "they never let me drive at the Vatican when I was a cardinal, and I'd really like to drive today."

"I'm sorry, Your Holiness, but I cannot let you do that. I'd lose my job! What if something should happen?" protests the driver, wishing he should have never gone to work that morning.

"Who's going to tell?" says the Pope with a smile.

Reluctantly, the driver gets in the back as the Pope climbs in behind the wheel. The driver quickly regrets his decision when, after exiting the airport, the Pontiff floors it, accelerating the limo to 205 km/hr. (Remember, the Pope is German)

"Please slow down, Your Holiness!" pleads the worried driver, but the Pope keeps the pedal to the metal until they hear sirens.

"Oh, dear god, I'm going to lose my license and my job!" moans the driver.

The Pope pulls over and rolls down the window as the cop approaches, but the cop takes one look at him, goes back to his motorcycle, and gets on the radio.

"I need to talk to the chief," he says to the dispatcher.

The chief gets on the radio and the cop tells him that he's stopped a limo going 205 km/hr.

"So bust him," says the chief.

"I don't think we want to do that, he's really important," said the cop.

The chief exclaimed, "All the more reason!"

"No, I mean really important," said the cop with a bit of persistence.

The chief then asked, "Who do you have there, the mayor?"

Cop: "Bigger."

Chief: "A senator?"

Cop: "Bigger."

Chief: "The Prime Minister?"

Cop: "Bigger."

"Well," said the chief, "Who is it?"

Cop: "I think it's God!"

The chief is even more puzzled and curious, "What makes you think it's God?"

Cop: "His chauffeur is the Pope!"

WHEN I SAY I'M BROKE— I'M BROKE

A little old lady answered a knock on the door one day, only to be confronted by a well-dressed young man carrying a vacuum cleaner.

"Good morning," said the young man. "If I could take a couple minutes of your time, I would like to demonstrate the very latest in high-powered vacuum cleaners."

"Go away!" said the old lady. "I'm broke and haven't got any money!" and she proceeded to close the door.

Quick as a flash, the young man wedged his foot in the door and pushed it wide open.

"Don't be too hasty!" he said. "Not until you have at least seen my demonstration."

And with that, he emptied a bucket of horse manure onto her hallway carpet.

"Now, if this vacuum cleaner does not remove all traces of this horse manure from your carpet, Madam, I will personally eat the remainder."

The old lady stepped back and said, "Well let me get you a fork, 'cause they cut off my electricity this morning."

Where Do Redheaded Babies Come From?

After their baby was born, the panicked father went to see the Obstetrician. "Doctor," the man said, "I don't mind telling you, but I'm a little upset because my daughter has red hair. She can't possibly be mine!"

"Nonsense," the doctor said. "Even though you and your wife both have black hair, one of your ancestors may have contributed red hair to the gene pool."

"It isn't possible," the man insisted. "This can't be, our families on both sides had jet-black hair for generations."

"Well," said the doctor, "let me ask you this. How often do you have sex?"

The man seemed a bit ashamed. "I've been working very hard for the past year. We only made love once or twice every few months."

"Well, there you have it!" The doctor said confidently.

"It's rust!"

WHY VEGAS IS NOT A SIN CITY

I TRULY DID NOT KNOW THIS!

LAS VEGAS CHURCHES ACCEPT GAMBLING CHIPS!

THIS MAY COME AS A SURPRISE TO THOSE OF YOU NOT LIVING IN LAS VEGAS, BUT THERE ARE MORE CATHOLIC CHURCHES THAN CASINOS.

NOT SURPRISINGLY, SOME WORSHIPERS AT SUNDAY SERVICES WILL GIVE CASINO CHIPS RATHER THAN CASH WHEN THE BASKET IS PASSED.

SINCE THEY GET CHIPS FROM MANY DIFFERENT CASINOS, THE CHURCHES HAVE DEVISED A METHOD TO COLLECT THE OFFERINGS.

THE CHURCHES SEND ALL THEIR COLLECTED CHIPS TO A NEARBY FRANCISCAN MONASTERY FOR SORTING AND THEN THE CHIPS ARE TAKEN TO THE CASINOS OF ORIGIN AND CASHED IN.

THIS IS DONE BY THE CHIP MONKS.

YOU DIDN'T EVEN SEE IT COMING DID YOU?

ABOUT LIVING

BRIDGES OF LIFE

Our life cannot always be full of happiness but it can always be full of love!

He who is blind to the view of our souls, will not enjoy and see life as it is.

The more you plan, the less likely you will experience chance, therefore live life to the fullest.

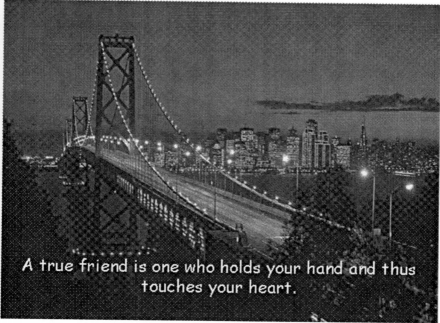

A true friend is one who holds your hand and thus touches your heart.

When we get married, we won't know what lies ahead
Until we hit the waves of life at sea.

Life is reality without an eraser!

Nothing in the future, will correct those moments that you have missed in the past.

Don't waste time with someone who won't support you in time of need.

Always look at the bright side of life. If there is no bright side, wait until the future turns to light.

Don't cry over what has happened in the past, but be happy that you could enjoy the moment.

Don't dispair, the nicest things will happen to you when you least expect them...

"Everything that happens, happens for a reason!"

CLUB 99

A truthful story that can all inspire us and make us realize that God blesses us with many favors—family, work, health, friends, salvation, joy, and peace that passes all understanding.

Contentment is the Key for all healing of heartaches that most people suffer. Let us begin to acknowledge that God will never give us trials and burdens that can just harm us and break us, but surely it will be the gateway to become a better person that He wants us to be and will give glorification to His name sake.

Club 99

Once upon a time, there lived a king who, despite his luxurious lifestyle, was neither happy nor content.

One day, the king came upon a servant who was singing happily while he worked. This fascinated the king; why was he, the supreme ruler of the land, unhappy and gloomy, while a lowly servant had so much joy. The king asked the servant, "Why are you so happy?"

The man replied, "Your Majesty, I am nothing but a servant, but my family and I don't need too much—just a roof over our heads and warm food to fill our tummies."

The king was not satisfied with that reply. Later in the day, he sought the advice of his most trusted advisor. After hearing the king's woes and the servant's story, the advisor said, "Your Majesty, I believe that the servant has not been made part of The 99 Club."

"The 99 Club? And what exactly is that?" the king inquired.

The advisor replied, "Your Majesty, to truly know what The 99 Club is, place 99 gold coins in a bag and leave it at this servant's doorstep."

When the servant saw the bag, he took it into his house. When he opened the bag, he let out a great shout of joy . . . So many gold coins!

He began to count them. After several counts, he was at last convinced that there were ninety-nine coins. He wondered, "What could've happened to that last gold coin? Surely, no one would leave ninety-nine coins!"

He looked everywhere he could, but that final coin was elusive. Finally, exhausted, he decided that he was going to have to work harder than ever to earn that gold coin and complete his collection.

From that day, the servant's life was changed. He was overworked, horribly grumpy, and castigated his family for not helping him make that hundredth gold coin. He stopped singing while he worked.

Witnessing this drastic transformation, the king was puzzled. When he sought his advisor's help, the advisor said, "Your Majesty, the servant has now officially joined The 99 Club."

He continued, "The 99 Club is a name given to those people who have enough to be happy but are never contented, because they're always yearning and striving for that extra one telling to themselves: 'Let me get that one final thing and then I will be happy for life.'"

We can be happy, even with very little in our lives, but the minute we're given something bigger and better, we want even more! We lose our sleep, our happiness, we hurt the people around us; all these as a price for our growing needs and desires. That's what "joining The 99 Club is all about."

. . . Now tell me are u part of the 99 club?

FLOWERS OF LIFE

The future belongs to those
who believe
in the beauty of their dreams."

Enjoy life,
this is not
a rehearsal.

"Think highly of yourself because the world takes you at your own estimate."

Don't fear pressure

for pressure is what turns rough stones into

diamonds

Live each day
in the present
and make it
beautiful.

"Believe
that your
life is worth
living

and your
beliefs will
help create
the fact."

Wherever you go,

take your whole heart

along.

"If you love life, life will love you back."

"Heal the past,
live the present,
dream the future."

"Don't count
the days
make the
days count."

The key to happiness is having dreams... The key to success is making dreams come true.

The world is like a mirror if you face it smiling, it smiles right back!

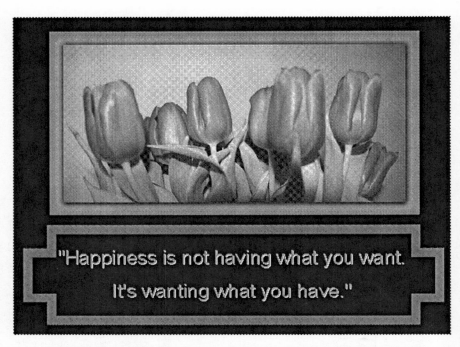

"Happiness is not having what you want. It's wanting what you have."

Learn to listen.
Opportunity sometimes knocks very softly.

"Life would be infinitely happier if we could only be born at the age of eighty and gradually approach eighteen."

Good times, become good memories. Bad times, become good lessons

It's not only
the scenery
you miss
by going
too fast ..

Succes is to get what you want ,
Luck is to keep what you get.

I look
to the future
because
that's where
I'm going to spend
the rest of
my life.

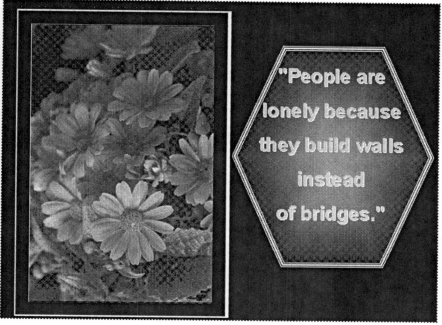

"People are
lonely because
they build walls
instead
of bridges."

Handy Hints

Peel a banana from the bottom and you won't have to pick the little stringy things off it. That's how the primates do it.

Take your bananas apart when you get home from the store.

If you leave them connected at the stem, they ripen faster.

Store your opened chunks of cheese in aluminum foil. It will stay fresh much longer and not mold!

Peppers with three bumps on the bottom are sweeter and better for eating. Peppers with four bumps on the bottom are firmer and better for cooking.

Add a teaspoon of water when frying ground beef. It will help pull the grease away from the meat while cooking.

To really make scrambled eggs or omelets rich, add a couple of spoonfuls of sour cream, cream cheese, or heavy cream and then beat them up.

For a cool brownie treat, make brownies as directed. Melt Andes mints in double broiler and pour over warm brownies. Let it set for a wonderful minty frosting.

Add garlic immediately to a recipe if you want a light taste of garlic and at the end of the recipe if you want a stronger taste of garlic.

Leftover snickers bars from Halloween make a delicious dessert. Simply chop them up with the food chopper. Peel, core, and slice a few apples. Place them in a baking dish and sprinkle the chopped candy bars over the apples. Bake at 350 for fifteen minutes! Serve alone or with vanilla ice cream. Yummm!

Heat up leftover pizza in a nonstick skillet on top of the stove, set heat to med-low and heat till warm. This keeps the crust crispy. No soggy micro pizza. I saw this on the cooking channel, and it really works.

For an easy Deviled Eggs, put cooked egg yolks in a zip lock bag. Seal, mash till they are all broken up. Add remainder of ingredients, reseal, keep mashing it up mixing thoroughly, and cut the tip of the baggy, squeeze mixture into egg. Just throw bag away when done easy clean up.

Expand Frosting. When you buy a container of cake frosting from the store, whip it with your mixer for a few minutes. You can double it in size. You get to frost more cake/cupcakes with the same amount. You also eat less sugar and calories per serving.

To reheat bread, biscuits, pancakes, or muffins that were refrigerated, place them in a microwave with a cup of water. The increased moisture will keep the food moist and help it reheat faster.

Newspaper weeds away. Start putting in your plants, work the nutrients in your soil. Wet newspapers, put layers around the plants overlapping as you go cover with mulch and forget about weeds. Weeds will get through some gardening plastic they will not get through wet newspapers.

To pick up broken glass, use a wet cotton ball or Q-tip to pick up the small shards of glass you can't see easily.

No More Mosquitoes. Place a dryer sheet in your pocket. It will keep the mosquitoes away.

Squirrel Away! To keep squirrels from eating your plants, sprinkle your plants with cayenne pepper. The cayenne pepper doesn't hurt the plant, and the squirrels won't come near it.

To have a flexible vacuum to get something out of a heat register or under the fridge, add an empty paper towel roll or empty gift wrap roll to your vacuum. It can be bent or flattened to get in narrow openings.

To reduce static cling, pin a small safety pin to the seam of your slip and you will not have a clingy skirt or dress. Same thing works with slacks that cling when wearing panty hose. Place pin in seam of slacks and . . . ta da . . . static is gone.

Before you pour sticky substances into a measuring cup, fill with hot water. Dump out the hot water, but don't dry cup. Next, add your ingredient, such as peanut butter, and watch how easily it comes right out.

Hate foggy windshields? Buy a chalkboard eraser and keep it in the glove box of your car When the window's fog, rub with the eraser! Works better than a cloth!

Reopen envelope. If you seal an envelope and then realize you forgot to include something inside, just place your sealed envelope in the freezer for an hour or two. Voila! It unseals easily.

Use your hair conditioner to shave your legs. It's cheaper than shaving cream and leaves your legs really smooth. It's also a great way to use up the conditioner you bought but didn't like when you tried it in your hair.

shutterstock - 1098266

Good-bye Fruit Flies. To get rid of pesky fruit flies, take a small glass, fill it 1/2 inch with Apple Cider Vinegar and two drops of dish washing liquid; mix well. You will find those flies drawn to the cup and gone forever!

Get Rid of Ants. Put small piles of cornmeal where you see ants. They eat it, take it home, can't digest it so it kills them. It may take a week or so, especially if it rains, but it works, and you don't have the worry about pets or small children being harmed!

Isn't It Strange?

Isn't it strange?

How a dollar bill seems like such a large amount when you donate it to church, but such a small amount when you spend it to for something else.

How an hour seem so long when you are in church and how short they seem when doing something else.

How hard to find words to say when you pray, but how easy to talk with somebody else.

How difficult to read a chapter in The Bible, but how easy to finish reading something else.

How we try and do whatever is possible to sit at the last row in church and whatever is possible to have a front row seat somewhere else!

How we put church last in our agenda, but we put first something else.

How sharing facts about God to others is not as interesting as sharing facts about something else.

How we question the words in the Bible, but believe right away on something else.

How everyone wants to go to heaven, but instead of doing things to get there they do something else.

How we think twice about forwarding e-mail messages about God but not about forwarding something else.

LIVE LIFE

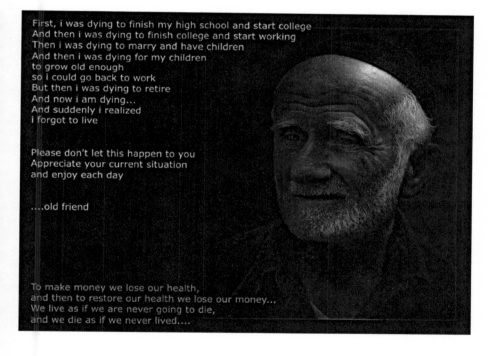

First, i was dying to finish my high school and start college
And then i was dying to finish college and start working
Then i was dying to marry and have children
And then i was dying for my children
to grow old enough
so i could go back to work
But then i was dying to retire
And now i am dying...
And suddenly i realized
i forgot to live

Please don't let this happen to you
Appreciate your current situation
and enjoy each day

....old friend

To make money we lose our health,
and then to restore our health we lose our money...
We live as if we are never going to die,
and we die as if we never lived....

Life is very short, so break your silly ego, forgive quickly, believe slowly, love truly, laugh loudly & never avoid anything that makes you smile.

When I woke up this morning lying in bed, I was asking myself;
what are some of the secrets of success in life?
I found the answer right there, in my very room . . .

The Fan said . . . Be cool
The Ceiling said . . . Aim high
The Window said . . . See the world
The Clock said . . . Every minute is precious
The Mirror said . . . Reflect
The Calendar said . . . Today is the beginning of the rest of your life
The Door said . . . Be part of the world

Carry a Heart that Never Hates.
Carry a Smile that Never Fades.
Carry a Touch that Never Hurts.

HAVE A BLESSED WORTHWHILE DAY!

SELF-ORGANIZATION FOR SUCCESS

Think about the most successful people you know for a moment.

For the most part, successful people are ruthless with their time. They take the time to do the inglorious task of planning. Getting and staying organized is grueling, but without it, you are on a collision course with failure.

A successful person self-organizes every day. Every Monday morning, he approached the week with confidence and enthusiasm. He is eager and anxious to see people because he had thought about them, studied their situations, and had some ideas he believed would be of value to them.

You may be thinking this isn't for you—you don't have time to devote a morning to planning—you don't want to be tied down to a schedule.

You are already living on a schedule and have a "To Do" list. And, if it's not properly planned, it's probably wasting time! One of the greatest satisfactions in life comes from getting things done and knowing you have done them to the best of your ability.

Do things in the order of their importance. Your enthusiasm and confidence will soar when you are organized!

- Designate a set period of time each week for self-organization, planning your week, getting things in order.
- Get up one hour earlier each day. Use this time to read and study.
- Keep your weekly and daily plans visible.

- Be ruthless with your time.
- Commit to bringing more order to your work and your personal life. The secret of freedom from anxiety over not having enough time lies not in working more hours, but in the proper planning of those hours.

REMEMBER: Each one of us have twenty-four hours a day. No one has more, no one has less. It is up to us how to spend those hours.

SIMPLE ADVICE FOR
A GOOD LIFE

An Angel says, "Never borrow from the future. If you worry about what may happen tomorrow and it doesn't happen, you have worried in vain. Even if it does happen, you have to worry twice."

- Pray.
- Go to bed on time.
- Get up on time so you can start the day unrushed.
- Say No to projects that won't fit into your time schedule.
- Delegate tasks to capable others.
- Simplify and unclutter your life.
- Less is more. (Although one is often not enough, two are often too many).
- Allow extra time to do things and to get to places.
- Pace yourself. Instead of doing all together, spread out difficult projects over time.
- Take one day at a time.
- Separate worries from concerns. For concerns, do what God would want you to do and let go of the anxiety. If you can't do anything about a situation, forget it.
- Live within your budget.
- Have backups—extra keys in your wallet, extra stamps, etc.
- KMS (Keep Mouth Shut) can prevent an enormous amount of trouble.
- Do something for the kid in you everyday.
- Carry a Bible wherever you go.
- Exercise and get enough rest.
- Eat right.

- Get organized so everything has its place.
- Write down thoughts and inspirations.
- Every day, find time to be alone.
- Talk to God on the spot. Don't wait until it's time to go to bed to try and pray.
- Make friends with Godly people.
- Keep a folder of favorite scriptures on hand.
- Remember that the shortest bridge between despair and hope is a "Thank you Jesus."
- Laugh.
- Laugh some more!
- Take your work seriously but not yourself at all.
- Develop a forgiving attitude (most people are doing the best they can).
- Be kind to unkind people (they probably need it the most).
- Sit on your ego.
- Talk less; listen more.
- Slow down.
- Remind yourself that you are not the general manager of the universe.
- Every night before bed, think of one thing you're grateful for that you've never been grateful for before. GOD HAS A WAY OF TURNING THINGS AROUND FOR YOU.

If God is for us, who can be against us?

(Rom. 8:31)

Stress Management

A lecturer, when explaining stress management to an audience, raised a glass of water and asked, "How heavy is this glass of water?" Answers called out ranged from 20-500 g.

The lecturer replied, "The absolute weight doesn't matter. It depends on how long you try to hold it. If I hold it for a minute, that's not a problem. If I hold it for an hour, I'll have an ache in my right arm. If I hold it for a day, you'll have to call an ambulance. In each case, it's the same weight, but the longer I hold it, the heavier it becomes."

He continued, "And that's the way it is with stress management. If we carry our burdens all the time, sooner or later, as the burden becomes increasingly heavy, we won't be able to carry on.

"As with the glass of water, you have to put it down for a while and rest before holding it again. When we're refreshed, we can carry on with the burden.

"So, before you return home tonight, put the burden of work down. Don't carry it home. You can pick it up tomorrow. Whatever burdens you're carrying now, let them down for a moment if you can."

So, my friend, why not take a while to just simply *relax*. Put down anything that may be a burden to you right now. Don't pick it up again until after you've rested a while. Life is short. Enjoy it!

Here are some great ways of dealing with the burdens of life:

*   Accept that some days you're the pigeon, and some days you're the statue.

* Always keep your words soft and sweet, just in case you have to eat them.

* Drive carefully. It's not only cars that can be recalled by their maker.

* If you can't be kind, at least have the decency to be quiet.

* If you lend someone $20 and never see that person again, it was probably worth it.

* It may be that your sole purpose in life is simply to be kind to others.

* Never put both feet in your mouth at the same time, because, then you won't have a leg to stand on.

* Nobody cares if you can't dance well. Just get up and dance.

* The second mouse gets the cheese.

* When everything's coming your way, you're in the wrong lane.

* Birthdays are good for you. The more you have, the longer you live.

* You may only be just one person in the world, but you may also be the whole world to one person.

* Some mistakes are too much fun to only make once.

* We could learn a lot from crayons—some are sharp, some are pretty, and some are dull. Some have weird names, and all are different colors, but they all have to live in the same box.

* A truly happy person is one who can enjoy the scenery on a detour.

THE 90/10 PRINCIPLE

Author: Stephen Covey

What is this principle?

10 percent of life is made up of what happens to you. 90 percent of life is decided by how you react . . .

What does this mean?

We really have *no* control over 10 percent of what happens to us. We cannot stop the car from breaking down. The plane will be arriving late, which throws off our whole schedule. A driver may cut us off in the traffic.

We have *no* control over this 10 percent.

The other 90 percent is different. You determine the other 90 percent.

How? . . . By your reaction.

You cannot control a red light. However, you can control your reaction. Do not let people fool you. You can control how you react.

Let us use an example.

You are having breakfast with your family. Your daughter knocks over a cup of coffee on your business shirt. You have no control over what has just happened. What happens next will be determined by how you react.

You curse. You harshly scold your daughter for knocking the cup over. She breaks down in tears. After scolding her, you turn to your wife, and you criticize her for placing the cup too close to the edge of the table. A short verbal battle follows.

You storm upstairs and change your shirt. Back downstairs, you find your daughter has been too busy crying to finish her breakfast and getting ready to go to school. She misses the bus. Your spouse must leave immediately for work. You rush to the car and drive your daughter to school.

Because you are late, you drive 40 miles per hour in a 30 mph speed limit zone. After a fifteen-minute delay and throwing $60.00 traffic fine away, you arrive at school. Your daughter runs into the building without saying good-bye.

After arriving at the office twenty minutes late, you realize you forgot your briefcase. Your day has started terrible. As it continues, it seems to get worse and worse. You look forward to coming home.

When you arrive home, you find a small wedge in your relationship with your wife and daughter.

Why? *Because of how you reacted in the morning.*

Why did you have a bad day?

A) Did the coffee cause it?
B) Did your daughter cause it?
C) Did the policeman cause it?
D) Did you cause it?

The answer is "D." You had no control over what happened with the coffee. How you reacted in those five seconds is what caused your bad day.

Here is what could have and should have happened.

Coffee splashes over you. Your daughter is about to cry.

You gently say: *"It's okay, honey, you just need to be more careful next time."*

Grabbing a towel, you go upstairs and change your shirt. You grab your briefcase, and you come back down in time to look through the window and see your child getting on the bus. She turns and waves. You arrive five minutes early to cheerfully greet the staff.

Notice the difference?

Two different scenarios: Both started the same. Both ended different.
Why? Because of how you reacted.

You really have no control over 10 percent of what happens in your life. The other 90 percent was determined by your reaction.

Here are some ways to apply the 90/10 principle.

If someone says something negative about you, do not be a sponge. Let the attack roll off like water on glass. You do not have to let the negative comments affect you.

React properly, and it will not ruin your day. A wrong reaction could result in losing a friend, being fired, or getting stressed out.

How do you react if someone cuts you off in the traffic? Do you lose your temper, pound on the steering wheel? *(a friend of mine had the steering wheel fall off),* Do you curse? Does your blood pressure skyrocket? Who cares if you arrive ten seconds later at work? Why let the cars ruin your drive?

Remember the 90/10 principle and don't worry about it.

You are told you lost your job. Why lose sleep and get irritated? It will work out. Use your worrying energy and time to find a new job.

The plane is late. It is going to mangle your schedule for the day. Why take out your frustration on the flight attendant? She has no control over what is going on. Use your time to study, get to know the other passengers, why stress out? It will just make things worse.

Now you know the 90/10 principle. Apply it, and you will be amazed at the results. You will lose nothing if you try it. The 90/10 principle is incredible. Very few know and apply this principle.

The result? You will see it by yourself! Millions of people are suffering from undeserved stress, trials, problems, and headaches. We all must understand and apply the 90/10 principle.
It can change your life!

. . . Enjoy it . . .

It only takes willpower to give ourselves permission to make the experience. Absolutely everything we do, give, say, or even think, it's like a boomerang. It will come back to us. If we want to receive, we need to learn to give first. Maybe we will end with our hands empty, but our heart will be filled with love. And those who love life, have that feeling marked in their hearts . . .

The End

THREE THINGS

Three Things

Three things in life
that can destroy a person
1. Anger
2. Pride
3. Unforgiveness

Three Things

Three things in life
that you should never lose
1. Hope
2. Peace
3. Honesty

Three Things

Three things in life
that are most valuable
1. Love
2. Family & Friends
3. Kindness

Three Things

Three things in life
that are never certain
1. Fortune
2. Success
3. Dreams

Three Things

Three things that make a person
1. Commitment
2. Sincerity
3. Hardwork

Three Gods

1. God The Father
2. God The Son
3. God The Holy Spirit

VACATION PLANS

There's that new beach in Japan . . .

Or the "Skywalk" at the Grand Canyon?

If you are not afraid of heights, there's "Tema park" in Las Vegas.

Or tennis at Dubai . . .

Like hiking?

Your Vacation Planner is brought to you by your friendly life insurance agent.

ABOUT MAN
AND
WOMAN

AN ANOMALY CALLED "WIFE"

I recently read that love is entirely a matter of chemistry. That must be why my wife treats me like toxic waste.

—*David Bissonette*

When a man steals your wife, there is no better revenge than to let him keep her.

—*Sacha Guitry*

After marriage, husband and wife become two sides of a coin; they just can't face each other, but still they stay together.

—*Hemant Joshi*

By all means marry. If you get a good wife, you'll be happy. If you get a bad one, you'll become a philosopher.

—*Socrates*

Woman inspires us to do great things, and prevents us from achieving them.

—*Dumas*

The great question which I have not been able to answer is—"What does a woman want?"

—*Sigmund Freud*

I had some words with my wife, and she had some paragraphs with me.

—*Anonymous*

Some people ask the secret of our long marriage. We take time to go to a restaurant two times a week, a little candlelight, dinner, soft music, and dancing. She goes Tuesdays, I go Fridays.

—*Henny Youngman*

I don't worry about terrorism. I was married for two years.

—*Sam Kinison*

There's a way of transferring funds that is even faster than electronic banking. It's called marriage.

—*James Holt McGavran*

I've had bad luck with both my wives. The first one left me and the second one didn't.

—*Patrick Murray*

Two secrets to keep your marriage brimming—
1. Whenever you're wrong, admit it,
2. Whenever you're right, shut up.

—*Nash*

The most effective way to remember your wife's birthday is to forget it once . . .

—*Anonymous*

You know what I did before I married? Anything I wanted to.

—*Henny Youngman*

My wife and I were happy for twenty years. Then we met.

—*Rodney Dangerfield*

A good wife always forgives her husband when she's wrong.

—*Milton Berle*

Marriage is the only war where one sleeps with the enemy.

—*Anonymous*

A man inserted an ad in the classifieds: "Wife wanted." Next day he received a hundred letters. They all said the same thing: "You can have mine."

—*Anonymous*

First guy (proudly): "My wife's an angel!"
Second guy: "You're lucky, mine's still alive."

—*Anonymous*

How Fights Start

My wife sat down on the settee next to me as I was flipping channels. She asked, "What's on TV?"

I said, "Dust."

And then the fight started . . . *

My wife and I were watching "Who Wants to Be a Millionaire" while we were in bed.

I turned to her and said, "Do you want to have sex?"

"No," she answered.

I then said, "Is that your final answer?"

She didn't even look at me this time, simply saying, "Yes."

So I said, "Then I'd like to phone a friend."

And then the fight started . . . *

Saturday morning I got up early, quietly dressed, made my lunch, and slipped quietly into the garage. I hooked up the boat up to the van, and proceeded to back out into a torrential downpour. The wind was blowing 50 mph, so I pulled back into the garage, turned on the radio, and discovered that the weather would be bad all day.

I went back into the house, quietly undressed, and slipped back into bed. I cuddled up to my wife's back, now with a different anticipation, and whispered, "The weather out there is terrible."

My loving wife of five years replied, "Can you believe my stupid husband is out fishing in that?"

And that's how the fight started . . . *

I rear-ended a car this morning. So, there we were alongside the road and slowly the other driver got out of his car.

You know how sometimes you just get soooo stressed and little things just seem funny? Yeah, well I couldn't believe it . . . He was a *dwarf!*

He stormed over to my car, looked up at me, and shouted, "*I am not happy!*"

So, I looked down at him and said, "Well, then which one are you?"

And then the fight started . . .

*

My wife was hinting about what she wanted for our upcoming anniversary.

She said, "I want something shiny that goes from 0 to 150 in about three seconds."

I bought her a bathroom scale.

And then the fight started . . . *

When I got home last night, my wife demanded that I take her some place expensive . . . so, I took her to a gasoline station.

And then the fight started . . .

After retiring, I went to the Social Security Office to apply for social security. The woman behind the counter asked me for my driver's license to verify my age. I looked in my pockets and realized I had left my wallet at home. I told the woman that I was very sorry, but I would have to go home and come back later.

The woman said, "Unbutton your shirt." So I opened my shirt revealing my curly silver hair.

She said, "That silver hair on your chest is proof enough for me" and she processed my Social Security application.

When I got home, I excitedly told my wife about my experience at the Social Security office.

She said, "You should have dropped your pants. You might have gotten disability, too."

And then the fight started . . . *

My wife and I were sitting at a table at my school reunion, and I kept staring at a drunken lady swigging her drink as she sat alone at a nearby table.

My wife asked, "Do you know her?"

"Yes," I sighed, "she's my old girlfriend. I understand she took to drinking right after we split up those many years ago, and I hear she hasn't been sober since."

"My God!" says my wife, "who would think, a person could go on celebrating that long?"

And then the fight started . . . *

I took my wife to a restaurant.

The waiter, for some reason took my order first. "I'll have the steak, medium rare, please."

He said, "Aren't you worried about the mad cow?"

"Nah, she can order for herself."

And then the fight started . . . *

A woman was standing nude, looking in the bedroom mirror.

She was not happy with what she saw and said to her husband, "I feel horrible; I look old, fat, and ugly. I really need you to pay me a compliment."

The husband replied, "Your eyesight's damn near perfect."

And then the fight started . . .

THE BLIND GIRL

There was a blind girl who hated herself because she was blind. She hated everyone, except her loving boyfriend. He was always there for her.

She told her boyfriend, "If I could only see the world, I will marry you."

One day, someone donated a pair of eyes to her. When the bandages came off, she was able to see everything, including her boyfriend.

He asked her, "Now that you can see the world, will you marry me?"

The girl looked at her boyfriend and saw that he was blind. The sight of his closed eyelids shocked her. She hadn't expected that. The thought of looking at them the rest of her life led her to refuse to marry him.

Her boyfriend left in tears and days later wrote a note to her saying: "Take good care of your eyes, my dear, for before they were yours, they were mine."

WOMAN AS EXPLAINED BY ENGINEERS

PART I

1 To find a woman you need Time and Money therefore:

$$Woman = Time \times Money$$

2 "Time is money" so

$$Time = Money$$

3 Therefore

$$Woman = Money \times Money$$

$$Woman = (Money)^2$$

4 "Money is the root of all problems"

$$Money = \sqrt{Problems}$$

5 Therefore

$$Woman = (\sqrt{Problems})^2$$

$$Woman = Problems$$

A⁺

PART II

 HAZARDOUS MATERIALS DATA SHEET

ELEMENT:	Woman
SYMBOL:	⚲
DISCOVERER:	Adam
ATOMIC MASS:	Accepted as 55kg, but known to vary from 45kg to 225kg

PHYSICAL PROPERTIES
1. Body surface normally covered with film of powder and paint
2. Boils at absolutely nothing – freezes for no apparent reason
3. Found in various grades ranging from virgin material to common ore

CHEMICAL PROPERTIES
1. Reacts well to gold, platinum and all precious stones
2. Explodes spontaneously without reason or warning
3. The most powerful money reducing agent known to man

COMMON USE
1. Highly ornamental, especially in sports cars
2. Can greatly aid relaxation
3. Can be a very effective cleaning agent

HAZARDS
1. Turns green when placed alongside a superior specimen
2. Possession of more than one is possible but specimens must never make eye contact

PART III

Chances of a Man Winning an Argument

PART IV

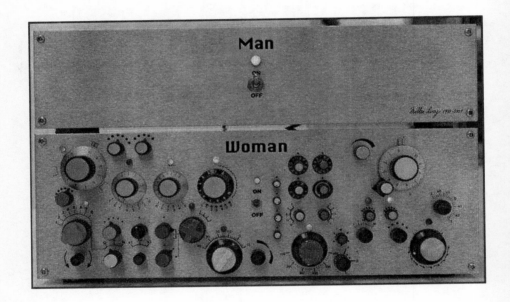

PART V

Mission: Go to Gap, Buy a Pair of Pants

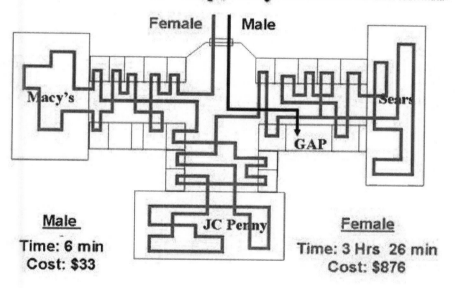

WORLD'S SHORTEST FAIRY TALE

Once upon a time, a guy asked a girl, "Will you marry me?"

The girl said, "No!"

The guy lived happily ever after and rode motorcycles and went fishing, hunting, and played golf a lot and drank beer and tequila, and had tons of money in the bank, and left the toilet seat up, and farted whenever he wanted.

The End

ABOUT PEOPLE

An American

Written by an Australian Dentist

You probably missed it in the rush of news last week, but there was actually a report that someone in Pakistan had published in a newspaper—an offer of a reward to anyone who killed an American, any American.

So an Australian dentist wrote an editorial the following day to let everyone know what an American is so they would know when they found one. (Good one, mate!)

An American is English, or French, or Italian, Irish, German, Spanish, Polish, Russian or Greek.

An American may also be Canadian, Mexican, African, Indian, Chinese, Japanese, Korean, Filipino, Australian, Iranian, Asian, Arab, Pakistani, or Afghan.

An American may also be a Comanche, Cherokee, Osage, Blackfoot, Navaho, Apache, Seminole, or one of the many other tribes known as Native Americans.

An American is Christian, or he could be Jewish, or Buddhist, or Muslim. In fact, there are more Muslims in America than in Afghanistan. The only difference is that in America they are free to worship as each of them chooses.

An American is also free to believe in no religion. For that, he will answer only to God, not to the government, or to armed thugs claiming to speak for the government and for God.

An American lives in the most prosperous land in the history of the world. The root of that prosperity can be found in the Declaration of Independence, which recognizes the God given right of each person to the pursuit of happiness.

An American is generous. Americans have helped just about every other nation in the world in their time of need, never asking a thing in return.

When Afghanistan was over-run by the Soviet army twenty years ago, Americans came with arms and supplies to enable the people to win back their country!

As of the morning of September 11, Americans had given more than any other nation to the poor in Afghanistan. Americans welcome the best of everything . . . the best products, the best books, the best music, the best food, the best services. But they also welcome the least.

The national symbol of America, The Statue of Liberty, welcomes your tired and your poor, the wretched refuse of your teeming shores, the homeless, tempest tossed. These in fact, are the people who built America.

Some of them were working in the Twin Towers the morning of September 11, 2001, earning a better life for their families. It's been told that the World Trade Center victims were from at least thirty different countries, cultures, and first languages, including those that aided and abetted the terrorists.

So you can try to kill an American if you must. Hitler did. So did General Tojo, and Stalin, and Mao Tse-Tung, and other blood-thirsty tyrants in the world. But, in doing so, you would just be killing yourself.

Americans are not particular people from a particular place. They are the embodiment of the human spirit of freedom. Everyone who holds to that spirit, everywhere, is an American.

ARE YOU COMPLAINING?

If you think you are unhappy, look at them.

If you think your salary is low, how about her?

When you feel like giving up, think of this man.

If you complain about your transport system, how about them?

If your society is unfair to you, how about her?

Are you still complaining?

Today before you say an unkind word—Think of someone who can't speak.

Before you complain about the taste of your food—Think of someone who has nothing to eat.

Before you complain about your husband or wife—Think of someone who's crying out to God for a companion.

Today before you complain about life—Think of someone who died too early on this earth.

Before you complain about your children—Think of someone who desires children but they're barren.

Before you argue about your dirty house someone didn't clean or sweep—Think of the people who are living in the streets.

Before whining about the distance you drive, Think of someone who walks the same distance with their feet.

And when you are tired and complain about your job—Think of the unemployed, the disabled, and those who wish they had your job.

But before you think of pointing the finger or condemning another—Remember that not one of us is without sin.

And when depressing thoughts seem to get you down—Put a smile on your face and think: you're alive and still around.

Life Is a Gift

MARRIAGE PROPOSALS

ACTUAL LETTER TAKEN FROM THE TIMES OF INDIA AS A RESPONSE TO A 'MARRIAGE PROPOSALS' ADVERTISEMENT!

MARRIAGE PROPOSAL IN PUNJABI ENGLISH (DON'T LAUGH; DEAD SERIOUS)

Madam:

I am an olden young uncle living only with myself in Lahore. Having seen your advertisement for marriage purposes, I decided to press myself on you and hope you will take me nicely. I am a soiled son from inside Punjab. I am nice and big, six foot tall, and six inches long. My body is filled with hardness, as because I am working hardly. I am playing hardly also.

Especially I like cricket, and I am a good batter and I am a fast baller. Whenever I come running in for balling, other batters start running. Everybody is scared of my rapid balls that bounce a lot. I am very nice man. I am always laughing loudly at everyone. I am jolly. I am gay. Ladies, they are saying I am nice and soft. Am always giving respect to the ladies.

I am always allowing ladies to get on top. That is how nice I am. I am not having any bad habits. I am not drinking and I am not sucking tobacco or anything else. Every morning I am going to the Jim and I am pumping like anything. Daily I am pumping and pumping. If you want you can come and see how much I am pumping the dumb belles in the Jim.

I am having a lot of money in my pants and my pants are always open for you. I am such a nice man, but still I am living with myself only. What to do? So I am taking things into my own hands everyday. That is why I am pressing myself on you, so that you will come in my house and my things into your hand.

If you are marrying me madam, I am telling you, I will be loving you very hard every day . . . fact, I will stop pumping dumb belles in the Jim. If you are not marrying me madam and not coming to me, I will press you and press you until you come. So I am placing my head between your nicely smelling feet looking up with lots of hope.

I am waiting very badly for your reply and I am stiff with anticipation.

Expecting soon yours and only yours,

Choudhary Warraich, born by mother in Okara and become big in Lahore, Punjab.

SCHOOL BUS IN PAKISTAN

ABOUT SAFETY

CREDIT CARD SCAM

Snopes.com says this is true. See this site *http://www.snopes.com/crime/warnings/creditcard.asp*.

This one is pretty slick since they provide you with all the information, except the one piece they want.

Note, the callers do not ask for your card number; they already have it. This information is worth reading. By understanding how the VISA and MasterCard Telephone Credit Card Scam works, you'll be better prepared to protect yourself.

One of our employees was called on Wednesday from VISA, and I was called on Thursday from Master Card.

The scam works like this:

Caller: "This is . . . (name), and I'm calling from the Security and Fraud Department at VISA. My Badge number is 12460. Your card has been flagged for an unusual purchase pattern, and I'm calling to verify. This would be on your VISA card, which was issued by (name of bank). Did you purchase an Anti-Telemarketing Device for $497.99 from a Marketing company based in Arizona?"

When you say *no*, the caller continues with, "Then we will be issuing a credit to your account. This is a company we have been watching and the charges range from $297 to $497, just under the $500 purchase pattern that flags most cards. Before your next statement, the credit will be sent to (gives you your address), is that correct?"

You say *yes*. The caller continues—"I will be starting a fraud investigation. If you have any questions, you should call the 1-800 number listed on the back of your card (1-800-VISA) and ask for Security."

You will need to refer to this control number. The caller then gives you a six digit number. "Do you need me to read it again?"

Here's the *important* part on how the scam works. The caller then says, "I need to verify you are in possession of your card." He'll ask you to turn your card over and look for some numbers. There are seven numbers; the first four are part of your card number, the next three are the security numbers that verify you are the possessor of the card. These are the numbers you sometimes use to make Internet purchases to prove you have the card. The caller will ask you to read the three numbers to him. After you tell the caller the three numbers, he'll say, "That is correct, I just needed to verify that the card has not been lost or stolen, and that you still have your card. Do you have any other questions?" After you say *no*, the caller then thanks you and states, "Don't hesitate to call back if you do have any," and hangs up.

You actually say very little, and they never ask for or tell you the card number. But after we were called on Wednesday, we called back within twenty minutes to ask a question. Are we glad we did! The *real VISA* Security Department told us it was a scam and in the last fifteen minutes a new purchase of $497.99 was charged to our card.

Long story—short—we made a real fraud report and closed the VISA account. VISA is reissuing us a new number. What the scammers want is the three-digit PIN number on the back of the card. Don't give it to them. Instead, tell them you'll call VISA or Master card directly for verification of their conversation. The real VISA told us that they will never ask for anything on the card as they already know the information since they have issued the card! If you give the scammers your three-digit PIN Number, you think you're receiving a credit. However, by the time you get your statement, you'll see charges for purchases you didn't make, and by then it's almost too late and/or more difficult to actually file a fraud report.

What makes this more remarkable is that on Thursday, I got a call from a Jason Richardson of Master Card with a word-for-word repeat of the VISA scam. This time I didn't let him finish. I hung up! We filed a police report, as instructed by VISA. The police said they are taking several of these reports daily! They also urged us to tell everybody we know that this scam is happening.

NEVER LIGHT A CANDLE IN AN AIR-CONDITIONED ROOM

Very Important: Never Light a Candle in an Air-Conditioned Room.

A friend in our group (Aramco Saudi) passed away last week due to carbon monoxide poisoning.

It happened when she lighted an aroma therapeutic candle for the night in a room with air conditioner *on*.

Due to lack of oxygen in the room, the burning of the candle cannot fully oxidize and thus form dangerous carbon monoxide.

Carbon monoxide will prevent oxygen exchange in the lungs, resulting in the person dozing off to a state of unconsciousness and eventually death in less than an hour, depending on the room size.

This e-mail is to make you aware of such danger when lighting aroma therapeutic candles in any unventilated rooms.

KEEP ASPRIN (325 MG) BY YOUR BEDSIDE

Recommended by American Heart Association

Why keep aspirin by your bedside?

About Heart Attacks!

There are other symptoms of a heart attack besides the pain on the left arm.

One must also be aware of an intense *pain on the chin*, as well as *nausea* and *lots of sweating*, although these symptoms may also occur less frequently.

Note: There *may be no pain in the chest* during a heart attack.

The majority of people (about 60 percent) who had a heart attack during their sleep did not wake up. However, if it occurs, the chest pain may wake you up from your deep sleep.

If you think you are having a heart attack, immediately **dissolve two aspirins in your mouth and swallow them with a bit of water.**

Then *CALL 911* immediately!

Also, phone a family member who lives very close by or a neighbor:

- Say **"heart attack!"**
- Say that you have taken two aspirins.
- Take a seat on a chair or sofa near the front door, and wait for their arrival and . . .

Do *not* lie down

GOOD VISION IN A DOWNPOUR

I don't know if this works but I am going to try it.

How to achieve good vision while driving during a heavy downpour?

I can vouch for this!

We are not sure why it is so effective; just try this method when it rains heavily. This method was told by a police friend who had experienced and confirmed it.

It is useful—even driving at night.

Most of the motorists would turn on *high* or *fastest speed* of the wipers during heavy downpour, yet the visibility in front of the windshield is still bad . . .

In the event you face such a situation, just try your *sun glasses* (any model will do), and miracle! All of a sudden, your visibility in front of your windshield is perfectly clear, as if there is no rain. Make sure you always have a pair of *sun glasses* in your car, as you are not only helping yourself to drive safely with good vision, but also might save your friend's life by giving him this idea . . .

SAFETY TIPS FOR WOMEN

This is not new, but I think it is worth sending as a reminder!!

Everyone should take five minutes to read this. It may save your life or your loved one's life.

Because of recent abductions in daylight hours, refresh you of these things to do in an emergency situation . . .

This is for you, and for you to share with your wife, your children, everyone you know. It never hurts to be careful in this crazy world we live in.

1. Tip from *Tae Kwon Do*: The elbow is the strongest point on your body. If you are close enough to use it, do!

2. If a robber asks for your wallet and/or purse, *do not hand it to him*. Toss it away from you . . . chances are that he is more interested in your wallet and/or purse than you, and he will go or the wallet/purse. *Run like mad in the other direction!*

3. If you are ever thrown into the trunk of a car, kick out the back tail lights and stick your arm out the hole and start waving like crazy. The driver won't see you, but everybody else will. This has saved lives.

4. Women have a tendency to get into their cars after shopping, eating, working, etc., and just sit (doing their checkbook, or making a list, etc.) *Don't do this!* The predator will be watching you, and this is the perfect opportunity for him to get in on the passenger side, put a gun to your head, and tell you where to go. *As soon as you get into your car, lock the doors and leave.*

If someone is in the car with a gun to your head, *Do not drive off*, repeat: *Do not drive off!* Instead, start the engine and speed into anything, wrecking the car. Your air bag will save you.

If the person is in the back seat, they will get the worst of it. As soon as the car crashes, get out and run. It is better than having them find your body in a remote location.

5. A few notes about getting into your car in a parking lot, or parking garage: Be aware: look around you, look into your car, at the passenger side floor, and in the back seat. If you are parked next to a big van, enter your car from the passenger door. Some serial killers attack their victims by pulling them into their vans while the women are attempting to get into their cars. Look at the car parked on the driver's side of your vehicle, and the passenger side. If a male is sitting alone in the seat nearest your car, you may want to walk back and get someone—guard or policeman to walk you back out.

It is always better to be safe than sorry. (And better paranoid than dead.)

6. *Always* take the elevator instead of the stairs. (Stairwells are horrible places to be alone and the perfect crime spot. This is especially true at *Night!*)

7. If the predator has a gun, and you are not under his control, *always run!* The predator will only hit you (a running target) four in hundred times; and even then, it most likely *will not* be a vital organ. *Run*, preferably in a zigzag pattern!

8. As women, we are always trying to be sympathetic: *Don't.* It may get you raped, or killed.

Ted Bundy, the serial killer, was a good-looking, well educated, man who *always* played on the sympathy of unsuspecting women. He walked with a cane, or a limp, and often asked 'for help' into his vehicle or with his vehicle, which is when he abducted his next victim.

9. Another Safety Point: Someone just told me that her friend heard a crying baby on her porch the night before last, and she called the police because it was late, and she thought it was weird. The police told her, "Whatever you do, *do not* open the door." The lady then said that it sounded like the baby had crawled near a window, and she was worried that it would crawl to the street and get run over. The policeman said, "We already have a unit on the

way, whatever you do, *do not open the door."* He told her that they think a serial killer has a baby's cry recorded and uses it to coax women out of their homes thinking that someone dropped off a baby. He said they have not verified it, but have had several calls by women saying that they hear baby's cries outside their doors when they're home alone at night.

Please pass this on and *do not* open the door for a crying baby—

The Crying Baby theory was mentioned on *America's Most Wanted* this past Saturday when they profiled the serial killer in Louisiana.

I'd like you to forward this to all the women you know. It may save a life. A candle is not dimmed by lighting another candle. I was going to send this to the ladies only, but guys, if you love your mothers, wives, sisters, daughters, etc., you may want to pass it onto them, as well.

BEWARE IN USING GPS AND MOBILE PHONES

This gives us something to think about with all our new electronic technology nowadays.

GPS

A couple of weeks ago, a friend told me that someone she knew had their car broken into while they were at a football game. Their car was parked on the green, which was adjacent to the football stadium and specially allotted to football fans.

Things stolen from the car included a garage door remote control, some money, and a GPS, which had been prominently mounted on the dashboard.

When the victims got home, they found that their house had been ransacked and just about everything worth anything had been stolen.

The thieves had used the GPS to guide them to the house. They then used the garage remote control to open the garage door and gain entry to the house.

The thieves knew the owners were at the football game, they knew what time the game was scheduled to finish, and so they knew how much time they had to clean up the house. It would appear that they had brought a truck to empty the house of its contents.

Mobile Phone

I never thought of this . . . This lady has now changed her habit of how she lists her names on her mobile phone after her handbag was stolen. Her handbag, which contained her cell phone, credit card, wallet, etc., was stolen.

Twenty minutes later, when she called her hubby, from a pay phone telling him what had happened, hubby says, "I received your text asking about our Pin number and I've replied a little while ago."

When they rushed down to the bank, the bank staff told them all the money was already withdrawn. The thief had actually used the stolen cell phone to text *hubby* in the contact list and got hold of the pin number. Within twenty minutes, he had withdrawn all the money from their bank account.

Moral of the lesson: Do not disclose the relationship between you and the people in your contact list. Avoid using names like Home, Honey, Hubby, Sweetheart, Dad, Mom, etc. And very importantly, when sensitive info is being asked through texts, *confirm* by calling back, not by texting.

Also, when you're being texted by friends or family to meet them somewhere, be sure to call back to confirm that the message came from them. If you don't reach them, be very careful about going places to meet family and friends who text you.

ACCIDENTAL POISONING

Taiwan, a woman suddenly died unexpectedly with signs of bleeding from her ears, nose, mouth, and eyes. After a preliminary autopsy, it was diagnosed death due to arsenic poisoning. Where did the arsenic come from?

The police launched an in-depth and extensive investigation. A medical school professor was invited to come to solve the case.

The professor carefully looked at the contents from the deceased's stomach, in less than half an hour the mystery was solved. The professor said, "The deceased did not commit suicide and neither was she murdered, she died of accidental death due to ignorance!"

Everyone was puzzled, why accidental death? The arsenic is of the U.S. Military for carrying rice seedlings H Gao. The professor said, "The arsenic is produced in the stomach of the deceased." The deceased used to take Vitamin C everyday, which in itself is not a problem. The problem was that she ate a large portion of shrimp/prawn during dinner. Eating shrimp/prawn is not the problem that's why nothing happened to her family even though they took the same shrimp/prawn.

However, at the same time the deceased also took vitamin C, which is where the problem is!

Researchers at the University of Chicago in the United States, found through experiments, food such as soft-shell shrimp/prawn contains a much higher concentration of five potassium arsenic compounds.

Such fresh food by itself has no toxic effects on the human body! However, in taking vitamin C, due to the chemical reaction, the original nontoxic five potassium

338

arsenic (As anhydride, also known as arsenic oxide, the chemical formula for As205) changed to a three potassium toxic arsenic (ADB arsenic anhydride), also known as arsenic trioxide, a chemical formula (As203), which is commonly known as arsenic to the public!

Arsenic poisoning have magma role and can cause paralysis to the small blood vessels, "mercapto Jimei," inhibits the activity of the liver and fat necrosis change Hepatic Lobules Centre, heart, liver, kidney, intestine congestion, epithelial cell necrosis, telangiectasia.

Therefore, a person who dies of arsenic poisoning will show signs of bleeding from the ears, nose, mouth, and eyes.

Therefore, as a precautionary measure, *do not eat* shrimp/prawn when taking vitamin C.

After reading this please do not be stingy. Forward to your friends and family!

ABOUT VIRTUE

MATHEMATICAL LOGIC

This comes from two math teachers with a combined total of seventy years experience.

Here is a little something someone sent me that is indisputable mathematical logic. It also made me laugh out loud.

This is a strictly mathematical viewpoint. It goes like this:

What Makes 100 percent? What does it mean to give *more* than 100 percent? Ever wonder about those people who say they are giving more than 100 percent? We have all been to those meetings where someone wants you to give over 100 percent. How about achieving 103 percent? What makes up 100 percent in life?

Here's a little mathematical formula that might help you answer these questions:

If:

A B C D E F G H I J K L M N O P Q R S T U V W X Y Z

is represented as:

1 2 3 4 5 6 7 8 9 10 11 12 13 14 15 16 17 18 19 20 21 22 23 24 25 26.

Then:

H-A-R-D-W-O-R-K
8 + 1 + 18 + 4 + 23 + 15 + 18 + 11 = 98%

and

K-N-O-W-L-E-D-G-E
11 + 14 + 15 + 23 + 12 + 5 + 4 + 7 + 5 = 96%

but,

A-T-T-I-T-U-D-E
1 + 20 + 20 + 9 + 20 + 21 + 4 + 5 = 100%

and,

B-U-L-L-S-H-I-T
2 + 21 + 12 + 12 + 19 + 8 + 9 + 20 = 103%

look how far ass kissing will take you.

A-S-S-K-I-S-S-I-N-G
1 + 19 + 19 + 11 + 9 + 19 + 19 + 9 + 14 + 7 = 127%

So, one can conclude with mathematical certainty, that While **Hard work** and **Knowledge** will get you close, and **Attitude** will get you there, its the **Bullshit** and **Ass kissing** that will put you over "the top."

"Remember some people are alive simply because it is illegal to shoot them"

Positive Attitude

John is the kind of guy you love to hate. He is always in a good mood and always has something positive to say. When someone would ask him how he was doing, he would reply, "If I were any better, I would be twins!"

He was a natural motivator. If an employee was having a bad day, John was there telling the employee how to look on the positive side of the situation. Seeing this style really made me curious, so one day I went up and asked him, "I don't get it! You can't be a positive person all of the time. How do you do it?"

He replied, "Each morning I wake up and say to myself, you have two choices today. You can choose to be in a good mood or you can choose to be in a bad mood. I choose to be in a good mood. Each time something bad happens, I can choose to be a victim or I can choose to learn from it. I choose to learn from it. Every time someone comes to me complaining, I can choose to accept their complaining or I can point out the positive side of life. I choose the positive side of life."

"Yeah, right, it's not that easy," I protested.

"Yes, it is," he said. "Life is all about choices. When you cut away all the junk, every situation is a choice. You choose how you react to situations. You choose how people affect your mood. You choose to be in a good mood or bad mood. The bottom line: It's your choice how you live your life."

I reflected on what he said. Soon hereafter, I left the Tower Industry to start my own business. We lost touch, but I often thought about him when I made a choice about life instead of reacting to it.

Several years later, I heard that he was involved in a serious accident, falling some sixty feet from a communications tower. After eighteen hours of surgery and weeks of intensive care, he was released from the hospital with rods placed in his back. I saw him about six months after the accident.

When I asked him how he was, he replied, "If I were any better, I'd be twins. Wanna see my scars?" I declined to see his wounds, but I did ask him what had gone through his mind as the accident took place. "The first thing that went through my mind was the well-being of my soon-to-be born daughter," he replied. "Then, as I lay on the ground, I remembered that I had two choices: I could choose to live or I could choose to die. I chose to live."

"Weren't you scared? Did you lose consciousness?" I asked.

He continued, " . . . the paramedics were great. They kept telling me I was going to be fine. But when they wheeled me into the ER and I saw the expressions on the faces of the doctors and nurses, I got really scared. In their eyes, I read 'he's a dead man.' I knew I needed to take action."

"What did you do?" I asked.

"Well, there was a big burly nurse shouting questions at me," said John. She asked if I was allergic to anything. "Yes," I replied. The doctors and nurses stopped working as they waited for my reply. I took a deep breath and yelled, "Gravity."

Over their laughter, I told them, "I am choosing to live. Operate on me as if I am alive, not dead."

He lived, thanks to the skill of his doctors, but also because of his amazing attitude . . . I learned from him that every day we have the choice to live fully. Attitude, after all, is everything.

Therefore, do not worry about tomorrow, for tomorrow will worry about itself. Each day has enough trouble of its own. (Matt. 6:34.)

After all, today is the tomorrow you worried about yesterday.

> Destiny is no matter of chance. It is a matter of choice. It is not a thing to be waited for, it is a thing to be achieved.
> —William Jennings Bryan

The Story of the Seed

Francis Kong

A successful businessman was growing old and knew it was time to choose a successor to take over the business. Instead of choosing one of his directors or his children, he decided to do something different. He called all the young executives in his company together.

He said, "It is time for me to step down and choose the next CEO. I have decided to choose one of you." The young executives were shocked, but the boss continued, "I am going to give each one of you a *seed* today—one very special *seed*. I want you to plant the seed, water it, and come back here one year from today with what you have grown from the seed I have given you. I will then judge the plants that you bring, and the one I choose will be the next CEO."

One man, named Jim, was there that day and he, like the others, received a seed. He went home and excitedly, told his wife the story. She helped him get a pot, soil, and compost and he planted the seed. Everyday, he would water it and watch to see if it had grown. After about three weeks, some of the other executives began to talk about their seeds and the plants that were beginning to grow.

Jim kept checking his seed, but nothing ever grew.

Three weeks, four weeks, five weeks went by, still nothing.

By now, others were talking about their plants, but Jim didn't have a plant, and he felt like a failure.

Six months went by—still nothing in Jim's pot. He just knew he had killed his seed. Everyone else had trees and tall plants, but he had nothing. Jim didn't say anything to his colleagues, however. He just kept watering and fertilizing the soil, he so wanted the seed to grow.

A year finally went by and all the young executives of the company brought their plants to the CEO for inspection. Jim told his wife that he wasn't going to take an empty pot.

But she asked him to be honest about what happened. Jim felt sick to his stomach, it was going to be the most embarrassing moment of his life, but he knew his wife was right. He took his empty pot to the boardroom. When Jim arrived, he was amazed at the variety of plants grown by the other executives. They were beautiful—in all shapes and sizes. Jim put his empty pot on the floor, and many of his colleagues laughed, a few felt sorry for him!

When the CEO arrived, he surveyed the room and greeted his young executives.

Jim just tried to hide in the back. "My, what great plants, trees, and flowers you have grown," said the CEO. "Today one of you will be appointed the next CEO!"

All of a sudden, the CEO spotted Jim at the back of the room with his empty pot. He ordered the financial director to bring him to the front. Jim was terrified. He thought, "The CEO knows I'm a failure! Maybe he will have me fired!"

When Jim got to the front, the CEO asked him what had happened to his seed. Jim told him the story.

The CEO asked everyone to sit down except Jim. He looked at Jim, and then announced to the young executives, "Behold your next Chief Executive Officer!

His name is Jim!" Jim couldn't believe it. Jim couldn't even grow his seed.

"How could he be the new CEO?" the others said.

Then the CEO said, "One year ago today, I gave everyone in this room a seed. I told you to take the seed, plant it, water it, and bring it back to me today. But I gave you all boiled seeds; they were dead; it was not possible for them to grow.

All of you, except Jim, have brought me trees and plants and flowers. When you found that the seed would not grow, you substituted another seed for the one I gave you. Jim was the only one with the courage and honesty to bring me a pot with my seed in it. Therefore, he is the one who will be the new Chief Executive Officer!"

End of story.

I have read variations of this story credited to anonymity but in terms of lesson is worth repeating specially in a country like ours that need to be reinforced with lessons on virtuous leadership.

Scriptures say whatsoever you sow you shall reap.

> Plant honesty and reap trust.
> Plant goodness and you reap friends.
> Plant humility and reap greatness.
> Plant perseverance and reap contentment.
> Plant consideration and reap perspective.
> Plant hard work and reap success.
> Plant forgiveness and reap reconciliation.
> Plant faith in *God* and reap a harvest.
> I guess the question is what are you planting now?

ABOUT THE WORLD

ANY COUNTRY NEEDS
A LEADER LIKE THIS

Prime Minister John Howard—Australia

Muslims who want to live under Islamic Sharia law were told on Wednesday to get out of Australia, as the government targeted radicals in a bid to head off potential terror attacks.

Separately, Howard angered some Australian Muslims on Wednesday by saying he supported spy agencies monitoring the nation's mosques. Quote:

"*Immigrants, not Australians, must adapt.* Take It or Leave It. I am tired of this nation worrying about whether we are offending some individual or their culture.

Since the terrorist attacks on Bali, we have experienced a surge in patriotism by the majority of Australians.

"This culture has been developed over two centuries of struggles, trials, and victories by millions of men and women who have sought freedom.

"We speak mainly *English*, not Spanish, Lebanese, Arabic, Chinese, Japanese, Russian, or any other language. Therefore, if you wish to become part of our society, learn the language!

"Most Australians believe in God. This is not some Christian, right wing, political push, but a fact, because Christian men and women, on Christian principles, founded this nation, and this is clearly documented. It is certainly appropriate to display it on the walls of our schools . . . If God offends you, then I suggest you consider another part of the world as your new home, because God is part of our culture.

"We will accept your beliefs, and will not question why. All we ask is that you accept ours, and live in harmony and peaceful enjoyment with us.

"This is OUR COUNTRY, OUR LAND, and OUR LIFESTYLE, and we will allow you every opportunity to enjoy all this . . . But once you are done complaining, whining, and griping about Our Flag, Our Pledge, Our Christian beliefs, or Our Way of Life, I highly encourage you take advantage of one other great Australian freedom, THE RIGHT TO LEAVE.

"If you aren't happy here then LEAVE. We didn't force you to come here. You asked to be here. So accept the country YOU accepted."

THE COUNTRY OF CHOICE

Are You Part of the Problem?

Will we still be the country of choice and still be America, if we continue to make the changes forced on us by the people from other countries that came to live in America because it is the Country of Choice?

Think about it! All we have to say is, when will they do something about *my rights*?

I celebrate Christmas, but because it isn't celebrated by everyone, we can no longer say Merry Christmas. Now it has to be Season's Greetings.

It's not Christmas vacation, it's winter break. Isn't it amazing how this winter break *always* occurs over the Christmas holiday?

We've gone so far the other way, bent over backward to not offend anyone, that I am now being offended. But it seems that no one has a problem with that.

This says it all! This is an editorial written by an American citizen, published in a Tampa, FL Newspaper. He did quite a job, didn't he? Read on, please!

Immigrants, Not Americans, Must Adapt.

I am tired of this nation worrying about whether we are offending some individual or their culture.

Since the terrorist attacks on Sept. 11, we have experienced a surge in patriotism by the majority of Americans. However, the dust from the attacks had barely settled when the *politically correct*! crowd began complaining about the possibility that our patriotism was offending others.

I am not against immigration, nor do I hold a grudge against anyone who is seeking a better life by coming to America.

Our population is almost entirely made up of descendants of immigrants. However, there are a few things that those who have recently come to our country, and apparently some born here, need to understand.

This idea of America being a multicultural community has served only to dilute our sovereignty and our national identity. As Americans, we have our own culture, our own society, our own language and our own lifestyle. This culture has been developed over centuries of struggles, trials, and victories by millions of men and women who have sought freedom.

We speak *English*, not Spanish, Portuguese, Arabic, Chinese, Japanese, Russian, or any other language.

Therefore, if you wish to become part of our society, learn the language!

"In God We Trust" is our national motto. This is not some Christian, right wing, political slogan. We adopted this motto because Christian men and women, on Christian principles, founded this nation . . . and this is clearly documented.

It is certainly appropriate to display it on the walls of our schools. If God offends you, then I suggest you consider another part of the world as your new home . . . because God is part of our culture.

If Stars and Stripes offend you, or you don't like Uncle Sam, then you should seriously consider a move to another part of this planet.

We are happy with our culture and have no desire to change, and we really don't care how you did things where you came from.

This is *our country*, our land, and our lifestyle. Our first amendment gives every citizen the right to express his opinion, and we will allow you every opportunity to do so!

But once you are done complaining . . . whining . . . and griping . . . about our flag . . . our pledge . . . our national motto . . . or our way of life, I highly encourage you to take advantage of one other great American freedom: *The Right to Leave.*

It is time for America to speak up!

THE PLAN

Robin Williams

Robin Williams, wearing a shirt that says "I love New York" in Arabic, made this speech in New York.

You gotta love Robin Williams—even if he's nuts! Leave it to Robin Williams to come up with the perfect plan. What we need now is for our UN Ambassador to stand up and repeat this message.

Robin Williams' plan . . . (It's hard to argue with this logic!)

"I see a lot of people yelling for peace but I have not heard of a plan for peace. So, here's one plan."

1. The United States will apologize to the world for our interference in their affairs, past and present. You know, Hitler, Mussolini, Stalin, Tojo, Noriega, Milosevic, Hussein, and the rest of those "good 'ole' boys," we will never interfere again.

2. We will withdraw our troops from all over the world, starting with Germany, South Korea, the Middle East, and the Philippines. They don't want us there. We would station troops at our borders. No one allowed sneaking through holes in the fence.

3. All illegal aliens have ninety days to get their affairs together and leave. We'll give them a free trip home. After ninety days the remainder will be gathered

up and deported immediately, regardless of whom or where they are. They're illegal! France will welcome them.

4. All future visitors will be thoroughly checked and limited to ninety days unless given a special permit! No one from a terrorist nation will be allowed in. If you don't like it there, change it yourself and don't hide here. Asylum would never be available to anyone. We don't need any more cab drivers or 7-11 cashiers.

5. No foreign students over age twenty-one. The older ones are the bombers. If they don't attend classes, they get a "D" and it's back home baby.

6. The United States will make a strong effort to become self-sufficient energy wise. This will include developing nonpolluting sources of energy but will require a temporary drilling of oil in the Alaskan wilderness. The caribou will have to cope for a while.

7. Offer Saudi Arabia and other oil producing countries $10 a barrel for their oil. If they don't like it, we go someplace else. They can go somewhere else to sell their production. (About a week of the wells filling up the storage sites would be enough.)

8. If there is a famine or other natural catastrophe in the world, we will not interfere. They can pray to Allah or whomever, for seeds, rain, cement, or whatever they need. Besides most of what we give them is stolen or given to the army. The people who need it most get very little, if anything.

9. Ship the UN Headquarters to an isolated island someplace. We don't need the spies and fair weather friends here. Besides, the building would make a good homeless shelter or lockup for illegal aliens.

10. All Americans must go to charm and beauty school. That way, no one can call us "Ugly Americans" any longer. The Language we speak is *English* . . . learn it . . . or *leave* . . . Now, isn't that a winner of a plan?

"The Statue of Liberty is no longer saying 'Give me your tired, your poor, your huddled masses." She's got a baseball bat and she's yelling, "you want a piece of me?"

THE CHANGING WORLD

Here is the speech of Geert Wilders, chairman, Party for Freedom, the Netherlands, at the Four Seasons, New York, introducing an Alliance of Patriots and announcing the Facing Jihad Conference in Jerusalem. The speech was sponsored by the Hudson Institute on September 25.

Dear friends,

Thank you very much for inviting me. Great to be at the Four Seasons. I come from a country that has one season only—a rainy season that starts on January 1 and ends December 31. When we have three sunny days in a row, the government declares a national emergency. So Four Seasons, that's new to me.

It's great to be in New York. When I see the skyscrapers and office buildings, I think of what Ayn Rand said: "The sky over New York and the will of man made visible." Of course, without the Dutch you would have been nowhere, still figuring out how to buy this island from the Indians. But we are glad we did it for you. And, frankly, you did a far better job than we possibly could have done.

I come to America with a mission. All is not well in the old world. There is a tremendous danger looming, and it is very difficult to be optimistic. We might be in the final stages of the Islamization of Europe. This not only is a clear and present danger to the future of Europe itself, it is a threat to America and the sheer survival of the West. The danger I see looming is the scenario of America as the last man standing. The United States as the last bastion of Western civilization, facing an Islamic Europe. In a generation or two, the United States will ask itself: who lost Europe? Patriots from around Europe risk their lives every day to prevent precisely this scenario form becoming a reality.

My short lecture consists of four parts.

First, I will describe the situation on the ground in Europe. Then, I will say a few things about Islam. Thirdly, if you are still here, I will talk a little bit about the movie you just saw. To close, I will tell you about a meeting in Jerusalem.

The Europe you know is changing. You have probably seen the landmarks. The Eiffel Tower and Trafalgar Square and Rome's ancient buildings and maybe the canals of Amsterdam, they are still there. And they still look very much the same as they did a hundred years ago. But in all of these cities, sometimes a few blocks away from your tourist destination, there is another world, a world very few visitors see and one that does not appear in your tourist guidebook. It is the world of the parallel society created by Muslim mass-migration. All throughout Europe, a new reality is rising: *entire Muslim neighborhoods where very few indigenous people reside or are even seen.*

And if they are, they might regret it. This goes for the police as well. It's the world of head scarves, where women walk around in figureless tents, with baby strollers, and a group of children. Their husbands, or slaveholders if you prefer, walk three steps ahead, with mosques on many street corners. The shops have signs you and I cannot read. You will be hard-pressed to find any economic activity. *These are Muslim ghettos controlled by religious fanatics.* These are Muslin neighborhoods, and they are mushrooming in every city across Europe. These are the building blocks for territorial control of increasingly larger portions of Europe, street by street, neighborhood by neighborhood, city by city.

There are now thousands of mosques throughout Europe. With larger congregations than there are in churches. *And in every European city, there are plans to build super-mosques that will dwarf every church in the region.* Clearly, the signal is: *we rule.*

Many European cities are already one-quarter Muslim: just take Amsterdam, Marseille, and Malmo in Sweden. In many cities, the majority of the under-18 population is Muslim. *Paris is now surrounded by a ring of Muslim neighborhoods.* Mohammed is the most popular name among boys in many cities. In some elementary schools in Amsterdam, the farm can no longer be mentioned, because that would also mean mentioning the pig, and that would be an insult to Muslims. *Many state schools in Belgium and Denmark only serve halal food to all pupils.* In once-tolerant Amsterdam, gays are beaten up almost exclusively by Muslims. Non-Muslim women routinely hear "whore, whore." *Satellite dishes are not pointed to local TV stations, but to stations in the country of origin.* In France, school teachers are advised to avoid authors deemed offensive to Muslims, including Voltaire and Diderot; the same is increasingly true of Darwin. The history of the Holocaust can in many cases no longer be taught because of Muslim sensitivity. *In England, sharia courts are now officially part of the British legal system.* Many neighborhoods in France are no-go areas for women without headscarves. Last week, a man almost died after being beaten up by Muslims in Brussels, because he was drinking during the Ramadan. Jews are fleeing France in record numbers, on the run for the worst wave of anti-Semitism since World War II. French is now commonly spoken on the streets of Tel Aviv and Netanya, Israel. I could go on forever with stories like this, stories about Islamization.

A total of fifty-four million Muslims now live in Europe. San Diego University recently calculated that a staggering 25 percent of the population in Europe will be Muslim just twelve years from now. *Bernhard Lewis has predicted a Muslim majority by the end of this century.*

Now, these are just numbers. And the numbers would not be threatening if the Muslim immigrants had a strong desire to assimilate. But there are few signs of that. The Pew Research Center reported that half of French Muslims see their loyalty to Islam as greater than their loyalty to France. One-third of French Muslims do not object to suicide attacks. The British Centre for Social Cohesion reported that one-third of British Muslim students are in favor of a worldwide caliphate. A Dutch study reported that half of Dutch Muslims admit they *understand* the 9/11 attacks.

Muslims demand what they call respect. And this is how we give them respect. Our elites are willing to give in, to give up. In my own country, we have gone from calls by one cabinet member to turn Muslim holidays into official state holidays, to statements by another cabinet member, that Islam is part of Dutch culture, to an affirmation by the Christian-Democratic attorney general that he is willing to accept sharia in the Netherlands, if there is a Muslim majority. We have cabinet members with passports from Morocco and Turkey.

Muslim demands are supported by unlawful behavior, ranging from petty crimes and random violence, for example against ambulance workers and bus drivers, to small-scale riots. Paris has seen its uprising in the low-income suburbs, the banlieues. Some prefer to see these as isolated incidents, but I call it a Muslim intifada. I call the perpetrators *settlers*, because that is what they are. *They do not come to integrate into our societies; they come to integrate our society into their Dar-al-Islam.* Therefore, they are settlers.

Much of this street violence I mentioned is directed exclusively against non-Muslims, forcing many native people to leave their neighborhoods, their cities, their countries.

Politicians shy away from taking a stand against this creeping sharia. They believe in the equality of all cultures.

Moreover, on a mundane level, Muslims are now a swing vote not to be ignored.

Our many problems with Islam cannot be explained by poverty, repression or the European colonial past, as the Left claims. Nor does it have anything to do with Palestinians or American troops in Iraq. *The problem is Islam itself.*

Allow me to give you a brief Islam 101. The first thing you need to know about Islam is the importance of the book of the Quran. The Quran is Allah's personal word, revealed by an angel to Mohammed, the prophet. This is where the trouble starts. *Every word in the Quran is Allah's word and therefore not open to discussion or interpretation.* It is valid for every Muslim and for all times. Therefore, there is no such a thing as moderate Islam. Sure, there are a lot of moderate Muslims. But a moderate Islam is nonexistent. *The Quran calls for hatred, violence, submission, murder, and terrorism. The Quran calls for Muslims to kill non-Muslims, to terrorize non-Muslims and to fulfill their duty to wage war: violent jihad. Jihad is a duty for every Muslim; Islam is to rule the world by the sword. The Quran is clearly anti-Semitic, describing Jews as monkeys and pigs.*

The second thing you need to know is the importance of Mohammed the prophet. His behavior is an example to all Muslims and cannot be criticized. Now, if Mohammed had been a man of peace, let us say like Gandhi and Mother Teresa wrapped in one, there would be no problem. But Mohammed was a warlord, a mass murderer, a pedophile, and had several marriages at the same time. Islamic tradition tells us how he fought in battles, how he had his enemies murdered, and even had prisoners of war executed.

Mohammed himself slaughtered the Jewish tribe of Banu Qurayza. He advised on matters of slavery, but never advised to liberate slaves. Islam has no other morality than the advancement of Islam. If it is good for Islam, it is good. If it is bad for Islam, it is bad. *There is no gray area or other side.*

Quran as Allah's own word and Mohammed as the perfect man are the two most important facets of Islam. Let no one fool you about Islam being a religion. Sure, it has a god, and a hereafter, and seventy-two virgins. But in its essence, Islam is a political ideology. It is a system that lays down detailed rules for society and the life of every person.

Islam wants to dictate every aspect of life. Islam means submission. *Islam is not compatible with freedom and democracy, because what it strives for is sharia.* If you want to compare Islam to anything, compare it to communism or national Socialism, these are all totalitarian ideologies.

This is what you need to know about Islam, in order to understand what is going on in Europe. For millions of Muslims, the Quran and the life of Mohammed are not fourteen centuries old, but are an everyday reality, an ideal, that guide every aspect of their lives. Now you know why Winston Churchill called Islam "the most retrograde force in the world," and why he compared Mein Kampf to the Quran, which brings me to my movie, Fitna.

I am a lawmaker, and not a moviemaker. But I felt I had the moral duty to educate about Islam. The duty to make clear that the Quran stands at the heart of what some people call terrorism, but is in reality, jihad. *I wanted to show that the problems of Islam are at the core of Islam, and do not belong to its fringes.*

Now, from the day the plan for my movie was made public, it caused quite a stir, in the Netherlands and throughout Europe. First, there was a political storm, with government leaders, across the continent, in sheer panic. The Netherlands was put under a heightened terror alert, because of possible attacks or a revolt by our Muslim population. The Dutch branch of the Islamic organization Hizb ut-Tahrir declared that the Netherlands was due for an attack. Internationally, there was a series of incidents. The Taliban threatened to organize additional attacks against Dutch troops in Afghanistan, and a Web site linked to Al Qaeda published the message that I ought to be killed, while various muftis in the Middle East stated that I would be responsible for all the bloodshed after the screening of the movie. In Afghanistan and Pakistan, the Dutch flag was burned on several occasions. Dolls representing me were also burned. The Indonesian president announced that I would never be admitted into Indonesia again, while the UN Secretary General and the European Union issued cowardly statements in the same vein as those made by the Dutch Government. I could go on and on. It was an absolute disgrace, a sell out. A plethora of legal troubles also followed, and have not ended yet. Currently the state of Jordan is litigating against me. Only last week there were renewed security agency reports about a heightened terror alert for the Netherlands because of Fitna.

Now, I would like to say a few things about Israel, because very soon, we will get together in its capital. *The best way for a politician in Europe to lose votes is to say something positive about Israel.* The public has wholeheartedly accepted the Palestinian narrative, and sees Israel as the aggressor. I, however, will continue to speak up for Israel. I see defending Israel as a matter of principle. I have lived in this country and visited it dozens of times. I support Israel. First, because it is the Jewish homeland after two thousand years of exile up to and including Auschwitz, second because it is a democracy, and third because *Israel is our first line of defense.*

Samuel Huntington writes it so aptly: "Islam has bloody borders." Israel is located precisely on that border. This tiny country is situated on the fault line of jihad, frustrating Islam's territorial advance. Israel is facing the front lines of jihad, like Kashmir, Kosovo, the Philippines, Southern Thailand, Darfur in Sudan, Lebanon, and Aceh in Indonesia. Israel is simply in the way. The same way West-Berlin was during the Cold War.

The war against Israel is not a war against Israel. It is a war against the West. It is jihad. Israel is simply receiving the blows that are meant for all of us. If there would have been no Israel, Islamic imperialism would have found other venues to release its energy and its desire for conquest. Thanks to Israeli parents who send their children to the army and lay awake at night, parents in Europe and America can sleep well and dream, unaware of the dangers looming.

Many in Europe argue in favor of abandoning Israel in order to address the grievances of our Muslim minorities. But if Israel were, God forbid, to go down, it would not bring any solace to the West. It would not mean our Muslim minorities would all of a sudden change their behavior, and accept our values. On the contrary, the end of Israel would give enormous encouragement to the forces of Islam. *They would, and rightly so, see the demise of Israel as proof that the West is weak, and doomed.* The end of Israel would not mean the end of our problems with Islam, but only the beginning. *It would mean the start of the final battle for world domination.* If they can get Israel, they can get everything.

Therefore, it is not that the West has a stake in Israel. It is Israel. It is very difficult to be an optimist in the face of the growing Islamization of Europe. All the tides are against us.

On all fronts we are losing. Demographically the momentum is with Islam. Muslim immigration is even a source of pride within ruling liberal parties. Academia, the arts, the media, trade unions, the churches, the business world, the entire political establishment have all converted to the *suicidal theory of multiculturalism*. So-called journalists volunteer to label any and all critics of Islamization as a "right-wing extremists" or "racists." The entire establishment has sided with our enemy. *Leftists, liberals, and Christian-democrats are now all in bed with Islam.*

This is the most painful thing to see: the betrayal by our elites. At this moment in Europe's history, our elites are supposed to lead us, to stand up for centuries of civilization, to defend our heritage, to honor our eternal Judeo—Christian values that made Europe what it is today. But there are very few signs of hope to be seen at the governmental level. Sarkozy, Merkel, Brown, Berlusconi—in private, they probably know how grave the situation is. But when the little red light goes on, they stare into the camera and tell us that Islam is a religion of peace, and we should all try to get along nicely and sing Kumbaya. They willingly participate in, what President Reagan so aptly called, "the betrayal of our past, the squandering of our freedom." If there is hope in Europe, it comes from the people, not from the elites. Change can only come from a grassroots level. It has to come from the citizens themselves. Yet these patriots will have to take on the entire political, legal, and media establishment.

Over the past years, there have been some small, but encouraging, signs of a rebirth of the original European spirit. Maybe the elites turn their backs on freedom, the public does not. In my country, the Netherlands, 60 percent of the population now sees the mass immigration of Muslims as the number one policy mistake since World War II. And another 60 percent sees Islam as the biggest threat to our national identity. I don't think the public opinion in Holland is very different from other European countries.

Patriotic parties that oppose jihad are growing, against all odds. My own party debuted two years ago, with 5 percent of the vote. Now it stands at 10 percent in the polls. The same is true of all military-minded parties in Europe. They are fighting the liberal establishment, and are gaining footholds on the political arena, one voter at the time.

Now, for the first time, these patriotic parties will come together and exchange experiences. It may be the start of something big, something that might change the map of Europe for decades to come. It might also be Europe's last chance.

This December a conference will take place in Jerusalem. Thanks to Professor Aryeh Eldad, a member of Knesset, we will be able to watch Fitna in the Knesset building and discuss the jihad. We are organizing this event in Israel to emphasize the fact that we are all in the same boat together, and that Israel is part of our common heritage. Those attending will be a select audience. No racist organizations will be allowed. And we will only admit parties that are solidly democratic. This conference will be the start of an Alliance of European Patriots. This alliance will serve as the backbone for all organizations and political parties that oppose jihad and Islamization. For this alliance, I seek your support.

This endeavor may be crucial to America and to the West. America may hold fast to the dream that, thanks to its location, it is safe from jihad and shaira. But seven years ago to the day, there was still smoke rising from ground zero, following the attacks that forever shattered that dream. Yet there is a danger even greater danger than terrorist attacks, the scenario of America as the last man standing. The lights may go out in Europe faster than you can imagine. An Islamic Europe means a Europe without freedom and democracy, an economic wasteland, an intellectual nightmare, and a loss of military might for America, as its allies will turn into enemies, enemies with atomic bombs. With an Islamic Europe, it would be up to America alone to preserve the heritage of Rome, Athens, and Jerusalem.

Dear friends, Liberty is the most precious of gifts. *My generation never had to fight for this freedom, it was offered to us on a silver platter, by people who fought for it with their lives. All throughout Europe, American cemeteries remind us of the young boys who never made it home, and whose memory we cherish. My generation does not own this freedom; we are merely its custodians. We can only hand over this hard won liberty to Europe's children in the same state in which it was offered to us. We cannot strike a deal with mullahs and imams.* Future generations would never forgive us. We cannot squander our liberties. We simply do not have the right to do so.

This is not the first time our civilization is under threat. We have seen dangers before. We have been betrayed by our elites before. They have sided with our enemies before. And yet, then, freedom prevailed. These are not times in which to take lessons from appeasement, capitulation, giving away, giving up, or giving in. These are not times in which to draw lessons from Mr. Chamberlain. *These are times calling us to draw lessons from Mr. Churchill and the words he spoke in 1942:*

> *"Never give in, never, never, never, never, in nothing great or small, large or petty, never give in except to convictions of honor and good sense. Never yield to force; never yield to the apparently overwhelming might of the enemy."*

WHAT A WONDERFUL WORLD

Louis Armstrong

the dark sacred night

And I think to myself...

Are also on the faces

of people going by

I watch them grow

They'll learn much more

Wanted: Associates From All Over The World

First of all, let me thank you for reading this book.

My main purpose for writing this book is to reach readers all over the world and be associated with them for my next books and other endeavors.

Let me get right to the point. If you like to make a difference on people's life, if you like writing, if you like being with people, if you like talking with people, if you are open minded, and if you are willing to listen to others about their stories, then I am inviting you to become my associate.

One God . . . one world . . . different people . . . different stories . . . Together, we can make the whole world learn and know those who make a difference.

Be one of the links. Join me. Be my associate.

Please express your interest in becoming my associate by emailing me at *Gerry@ Grindulo.com* with a brief description of your self.

Once again, thank you very much.

Gerry G. Grindulo
Author and Founder of *The Difference*

Breinigsville, PA USA
23 May 2010
238500BV00002B/2/P